☑ **W9-CCC-008**

THE FOUR JAMESES

THE FOUR JAMESES
William Arthur Deacon
Introduction by Doug Fetherling

MACMILLAN/TORONTO

© *William Arthur Deacon 1953*

Introduction © *Doug Fetherling 1974*

All rights reserved. The use of any part of this
publication reproduced, transmitted in any form or
by any means, electronic, mechanical, photocopying,
recording, or otherwise, or stored in a retrieval
system, without the prior consent of the publisher
is an infringement of copyright law.

ISBN 0-7705-1153-8

First published 1927   Ryerson Press edition 1953   This edition 1974

Acknowledgement is made to McGraw-Hill Ryerson Limited
for permission to reproduce the Ryerson Press edition of
The Four Jameses.

Printed in Canada for
The Macmillan Company of Canada, Limited
70 Bond Street, Toronto M5B 1X3

Contents

Introduction by Doug Fetherling

The Four Jameses by William Arthur Deacon is that rare thing in Canadian literature: an underground classic. When it was first published, in 1927, by Graphic Publishers of Ottawa, the pioneer commercial literary press in this country, it was found to be one of those curiosities of literature that goes on steadily from year to year, resuscitated by word of mouth just when it seems to be expiring. Testament to this is the fact that during the Depression when Graphic had gone out of business and most of its books had passed into literary receivership (one possible exception is Grove's *A Search for America*), the unbound sheets of *The Four Jameses* were purchased and distributed in paper wrappers. These copies, like the original clothbound ones, were prized, for this is the kind of book one never disposes of when moving. The work continued to gain each year a few fans who had had it recommended to them or who stumbled upon it, until 1953, when Deacon reissued it in slightly revised form and with additional chapters for a new generation who accorded it similar status. It is the text of this Ryerson Press edition that is issued again here to rekindle interest in this small masterpiece that has been passed hand to hand, lent out and hired through a devoted underground that has revelled in its wit and malicious grace.

It is particularly appropriate that *The Four Jameses* should reappear at this moment in our history when, it seems to me, although many literary nationalists are doing fine things for our cultural health, many others are boring us with their humourless manifestos and trite ultimatums. The beauty of Deacon, and it is most obvious in this his most unified work, is

7

that while a landmark cultural nationalist, he had a sly sense of fun that set him apart by allowing him to see and point out the humour in what was at once both Canadian and dreadful. It is these two qualities, nationality and sheer lack of talent, that make the four Jameses — the poets James McIntyre, James Gay, James MacRae, and James Gillis — hold together as a group. In treating them seriously, Deacon was making fun of them and others like them; though he treated them as gently as he usually did those he was compelled to criticize in his almost half-century of literary commentating. But he also was making fun of a style of genteel criticism and of academic critics who made up (and still make up) for their lack of ideas by seeking out bottom-of-the-barrel discoveries seldom worth the trouble, and then surveying them with obtuse phrases which only further betray their reticence about thinking. If anyone else, however, had written *The Four Jameses* those forty-six years ago, it would have been the work of a dilettante who had not put his money where his mouth was. Alone among Canadians of his time, Deacon was the writer who had done enough to justify his sitting back and making light of domestic poetasters, tea-sipping literary ladies, professors — and himself.

William Arthur Deacon was born in 1890 in Pembroke, Ontario, and took arts courses at various schools in the east, though he eventually took a law degree from the University of Manitoba in 1918. That same year he began practising in Winnipeg, though his literary inclinations soon gained control and made the law seem boring. In 1921, while still with the firm of Pitblado and Co., Barristers and Solicitors, he accepted the honorary position of assistant literary editor of the *Winnipeg Free Press* and the next year became literary editor of *Saturday Night* in Toronto, writing reviews, obituaries, sketches, and (at his editor's insistence?) a series of weekly legal pieces. This was the periodical that over the years has sheltered its share of men of letters — Hector Charlesworth, B. K. Sandwell, Robertson Davies, and Robert Fulford among them — and Deacon was not the least important. He too left his mark on the magazine, for in 1925 he established the *Saturday Night* book review section. He stayed on until 1928, when he left to become book editor of the Toronto *Mail and Empire,* which merged with the *Globe* to become the *Globe and Mail* in 1936.

Still a relatively young man, Deacon arrived at the paper with most of his books, and all his important ones, already behind him. Not only *The Four Jameses* but two earlier collections of serio-comic essays, *Pens and Pirates* (Ryerson, 1923) and *Poteen* (Graphic, 1926), in which one sees now the talent and style that wanted only the parody form and later polish to produce this more durable book. With his regular reviews (these quickly developed into his column "The Fly Leaf", which he continued after his retirement until 1963) he became Canada's first full-time professional reviewer, secure in a base of operations for which his work up to that time had helped prepare him.

It had begun in Winnipeg in 1918 when he had written to the *New York Times Book Review* about a title it had neglected to mention and enclosed modestly his own comments. These were printed, and Deacon received a cheque for ten dollars. Later he contributed to many Canadian, British, and American publications, including among the latter the *Saturday Review of Literature* (as it then was) and the *American*

Mercury, edited respectively by his friends and correspondents Henry Seidel Canby and H. L. Mencken. Both taught him a great deal, but in *The Four Jameses,* his most mature work, the influence of the *Mercury* is the stronger, as it became in his writing generally and in his personality. "Surely the capable and honest critic would not be tendered a banquet," he said when just that was happening to him shortly after his retirement from the *Gloge and Mail* in 1960. "He would be hated and reviled — possibly stoned. Wherein have I failed?"

It was contradictory, for he had been all those years capable and forthright, but it was also very funny. It sounded like something Mencken would have said and posibly did say. Mencken's partner, George Jean Nathan, expressed similar thoughts on several occasions. The three were something alike in their voices, though Mencken's and Nathan's were livelier and harsher and farther-reaching. Deacon's was gentle, at times almost imploring, but never without his humour and his common sense. It is this common sense that really is the strongest link with his peers abroad, this and the fact Deacon, like them, was a great mover and shaker of writers. Perhaps he was even the greater one. Certainly, since firmly established writers were so pitifully few in Canada, he was the most needed, and he met his mandate, tirelessly banging away at native pendantry and puritanism while doing the great deal in his power to foster Canadian writing with a clear head.

Deacon was perhaps the first important English-Canadian man of letters, in the sense of a journalistic writer whose work, while literary, is not usually imaginative. And it was almost exclusively literary and largely Canadian. Though of necessity his writings crossed the line sometimes into social issues, as the good critic's do — he wrote a free-press pamphlet *Here Comes*

INTRODUCTION

the Censor in 1940 and the nationalist *My Vision of Canada* in 1933, a brave critique by that day's standards, an optimistic one by this day's — he stuck pretty close to the job of improving the quality of literary life. In "The Fly Leaf" he cajoled and pontificated ("through a cloud of pipe smoke", one colleague said), and he carried on a voluminous correspondence in addition to speaking at almost every opportunity in criticism and in defence of our then struggling literary world.

He was one of the founders of the Canadian Authors Association in 1922 and over the years held numerous offices, including that of national president. If today that much-maligned collection of little old ladies of both sexes has small relevance, it must be remembered that then and for a few years it included real as well as amateur authors, and the crime charged Deacon should only be that, in his optimism for a healthy community, he was overzealous in the breadth of his criteria for exclusion and slow in his realization of what was happening to a rather good idea. Deacon had a hand also in the Toronto chapter of P.E.N. in the late twenties and early thirties, during which period he was also involved in the Toronto Writers Club. From this group sprang the 1931 essay collection *Open House,* which Deacon edited with Wilfred Reeves and which included work by his friends Merrill Denison, Roy Greenaway, Charles G. D. Roberts, and E. J. Pratt, a disparate bunch of writers held together by nothing so much as their will to survive in a hostile climate and even to seek the warmth of an artificial gentility.

With Deacon no less than with the rest (even Greenaway and the other rough-hewn newspapermen), it is this last quality that makes them seem dated today and that affected sometimes their literary judgement. But let us not in Deacon's case confuse his contribution with his vagaries of taste imposed by his not wanting to emulate America and his knowledge that England was too far away to matter much. He wrote a praising monograph on Peter MacArthur for his friend Lorne Pierce's "Makers of Canadian Literature" series, true; but he gave a lecture course, before anyone else really thought to, on the rise of Canadian literature; he founded the Governor General's awards committee and kept it alive; and in his work with the Wartime Prices and Trade Board prevented the government from rationing paper for books. Morever, he wrote reviews, talked, listened, read, and contributed to anthologies with such energy as to inspire energy in others, and that is part of the man of letters' job.

The Four Jameses operates on several planes of humour. The most obvious is the title itself, with its sonorous echo of *The Four Georges,* Thackeray's lives of the monarchs. Then there is the twofold mocking of Deacon himself. First, he is taking a poke at his weakness as a frequent proponent of tweedy Christopher Morley-type criticism, a monster he followed but did not create. Secondly, he is making light of his strength as a literary nationalist, with the implication that these idiotic *poètes manqués* were somehow indigenous Canadian creatures reflecting something basic to the national character. Actually, as he well knew, they were the standard or substandard talentless imitators of the Tennysonian school, a plague that covers the west without regard for frontiers. Deacon pretends to see them as poets meeting the challenge of the industrial age and pretends to side with them in their view of themselves as geniuses without honour in their own or any other land. Throughout there is little hint of the poets as the common eccentrics they were.

INTRODUCTION

Deacon keeps a straight face when he quotes James Gay, the second most abominable of the writers, and his message to Tennyson: "Now Longfellow is gone [and] there are only two of us left." Deliberately he makes no reference to the equally glandular egos who called themselves poets, such as the Victorian Scot, the Great MacGonagall, most famous of them all, whose autobiography begins "Like most great men, I was born at a very early period of my existence . . . " and who distributed business cards reading:

WM. MacGonagall

SUCCESSOR TO

WM. SHAKESPEARE.

Poetry Executed on the Shortest Notice.

MacGonagall it is who most resembles James McIntyre, the best known of the four Jameses partly through the efforts of a Toronto journalist who thrice, by my count, has scalped Deacon's survey for magazine and newspaper pieces, often as not confusing the facts. Does not McIntyre's "Ode on the Mammoth Cheese" (which would be his stock anthology piece were he ever in anthologies), the one beginning

> We have seen thee, queen of cheese
> Lying quietly at your ease,
> Gently fanned by evening breeze,
> Thy fair form no flies dare seize. . . .

does not this resemble MacGonagall's no less well-known ode "The Newport Railway"?

> Success to the Newport Railway,
> Along the braes of the Silvery Tay
> And to Dundee straightaway.
> Across the railway bridge o' the Silvery Tay
> Which was opened on the 12th of May,
> In the year of our Lord 1879. . . .

In truth, there were and are scores of such persons in addition to these outlandish Canadians who make the invention of Sarah Binks seem redundant. In his memoirs, the Boston bookseller Charles Goodspeed defined their work as that of "unconscious humor, the products of abnormal minds and marked by eccentricities of structure, by inconsequence, or by incoherent thought" but distinguished from that of Tennyson and others, the "writers ordinarily sane who at some time have written poetry which has one or more of these peculiarities". Goodspeed's list included a number of New England equivalents of McIntyre, Gay, and the rest as well as the awful Bloodgood H. Cutter, Long Island farmer-poet, and the storied Julia A. Moore, Sweet Singer of Michigan.

Such rhymesters in fact seem to appeal to a special type of bookseller, which Deacon might easily have become had he not been so much a writer. The Anglo-American rare-book dealer David Magee himself collects these works, including Moore's, and the breed has even come under the study of the erudite David A. Randall, now of the Lilly Library. The difference between their bookseller-layman's interest and William Arthur Deacon's writer's interest is the extent to which Deacon dwells on the poets' personalities and makes them live again, however ludicrously. As he writes in *The Four Jameses* (page

115) when comparing Gillis's *Cape Breton Giant* with Carlyle's *French Revolution,* "it is the personality of the author that counts in bellelettristic writing." Deacon gives us five personalities in this study of four Jameses. It is his own that rings truest and that would remain alive alone were it not mixed so inextricably in this book with those of other men who so deserve to be forgotten but who so fortunately are not.

N.B. The bibliography from the 1953 edition is retained as a library guide and as a further example of Deacon's concern with the subjects of *The Four Jameses.* All the titles are out of print at this writing, and the addresses listed are no longer valid in these contexts. One addition to the list, however, comes with the discovery, by Toronto book dealer David Mason, of copies of McIntyre's *Poems* (1889) bound with his hitherto unlisted work, *The Rise of the Canadian Cheese Trade and Descriptive Poems and Tales* (1891?). Apparently McIntyre caused to be bound with the new work the unsold sheets of the old. Books by all four Jameses are in demand as curios and are often catalogued by Canadian dealers at weighty prices.

THE FOUR JAMESES

The Royal Line

THACKERAY'S REASONS FOR WRITING *The Four Georges* were very different from mine in undertaking *The Four Jameses,* even as eighteenth century England differed from nineteenth century Canada, and the throne of a great state differs from the modest yet potent kingdom of letters. But I will not admit that his subjects were more important than mine, nor one half as interesting. After introducing my monarchs of the quill individually, I shall have more to say about their significance as a dynasty.

The works of Gay and McIntyre have long been out of print; and though the books of neither are as rare as some writers have asserted, there is still a real demand for their poems that is not being met. Gillis's and MacRae's volumes are on the market; and it is my hope to introduce these to persons who would value them as permanent additions to their libraries. I found, too, that many readers rejoiced in the writings of one of these men without having heard of the others. It is my hope to lead the lovers of Gay to take up the study of Gillis, and the worshippers of McIntyre to look into MacRae. If a form of reciprocity can be set up, whereby Gillis attains in Ontario the popularity he has long enjoyed in the East, and the book lovers of the

Maritimes in exchange begin to patronize Gay and McIntyre, my labors will not have been in vain, to say nothing of the education of Westerners respecting all four worthies.

Another incentive was my alarm over the possibility of these poets becoming legendary figures through lack of biographical attention; and the fear that future generations might know no more of them than we do of Homer, and ascribe their very individual efforts to folk or group production. Surprising as it may seem in these days, when every petty official has at least one book devoted to his life, no previous researches have been made into the personal histories of these four diverse and picturesque writers, except the most superficial studies, resulting in entirely inadequate magazine and newspaper articles.

My sketches of the authors' lives are not as full as I would like; but they are the most extensive yet published, bringing to light many suggestive facts not previously printed. In directing attention to these gentlemen and their careers as fit subjects for further research, I believe I have performed a public service; and I crave the indulgence of my readers until a second edition supplies whatever corrections and additions may be found necessary.

The generous quotations are due in part to the lack of present facilities for obtaining some of the books from which they are drawn, and with the hope of forcing out new complete editions; and in part to the need I felt for some sort of anthology, to emphasize the quantity of this material available in this country to those who have the patience to unearth it.

In conclusion, I wish to assure my readers that I have been inspired by altruistic motives. These writers have afforded me pleasure for many years: it is my aim to assist others to partake of the same joy in the most convenient and agreeable manner.

James Gay : Poet Laureate of Canada, and Master of All Poets

I.—HIS LIFE

What is man, poor sinful man, or any of his race,
Without a greater power to keep him in his place?
We are nothing of ourselves, here we cannot stay;
Then read the noble writings of the Poet James Gay.

FIRST IN POINT OF TIME OF THE ILLUSTRIOUS AUTHORS, whose fame it is my privilege to perpetuate in this volume, James Gay was also the first to attain an international reputation. So it is quite fitting that he should have assumed the title of laureate; and everyone must deeply regret that he did not get from the Dominion Government the medal for which he frequently petitioned.

We learn from *My Address to Her Majesty* that the cities of Guelph and Belleville had medals struck for him; and we can only blame the prosaic nature of Sir John A. Macdonald and the cabinet ministers of his administration, and their blindness to the distinction conferred upon a country by the residence in it of a literary genius, for their failure to honor Gay officially. Alas! it is one of the blunders that can never be

21

repaired since the old man has been nearly forty years in his grave. Our distress over the knowledge that his declining years were not brightened by receipt of the coveted medal is only tempered by the fact that continued disappointment led him to compose additional addresses to Queen Victoria and the then Governor-General of Canada; and who can wish whole-heartedly for anything that might have deprived the world of a single line from his pen?

The title he wisely took, without asking anybody's permission. He wore it proudly and unchallenged. Indeed, until Bliss Carman's crowning at Montreal in 1921 (likewise unofficial) no Canadian poet has ever aspired to the laureateship—so profound an impression did Gay make as first wearer of the honor.

Unfortunately, he won fame too late in life for any one to realize the importance of keeping biographical records. For details of his life we are almost wholly dependent upon the happily frequent autobiographical allusions in his poems. These may be relied upon as accurate, since Gay took himself and his career so seriously that it would be foolish to suppose that the poetic license, which is the distinguishing characteristic of his work as a whole, would be allowed to interfere with the factual accuracy of any information about himself.

James Gay was born on March 24, 1810, at Bratton,

Clovelly, Devonshire, England, about twelve miles from Barnstaple, the birth-place of John Gay (1685-1732), a playwright and poet most generally remembered for *The Beggar's Opera*. No blood relationship has yet been traced between the two men; but the English habit of a family remaining in one district through many generations gives some justification for supposing the two Gay poets to have sprung from a common stock.

Of James Gay's education no particulars have been preserved, but internal evidence indicates that the influences of his early home life made for piety and simple honesty. It is unlikely that elaborate educational facilities were available to the young genius, since he speaks of his home as a "thatched cot," and universities were then only for the wealthy. Besides, the freedom of his compositions from deformities resulting from the cramping rules of grammar was probably only possible to one who had escaped the severer forms of a classical education. Thus Providence saw to it that the poet's formative years should be unhampered by stale conventions, to the end that his talents might develop that originality for which his name will always be remembered.

His strong leanings toward pacifism, coupled with sturdy independence of thought, rather point to a Quaker upbringing, though he was a member of the

Church of England. He seems to have attended the Baptist Church in his Canadian home, for we find in *A Friendly Advice to the Baptist People* the lines:

> When I first went to your church
> It was all very small, and yet there was room.

His disapproval of sectarianism would certainly have drawn him—had he lived long enough—into the ranks of The United Church of Canada.

> The best-learnt man on earth cannot fathom the different propen-
> sities of man,
> As their differences in their belief is almost numerous as the sand.

Also:

> Nothing greater could ever please me,
> To see all churches in Guelph unite and agree.

Love of Nature, subordinated in the poems of his maturity to humanitarian and philosophical themes, was present in youth, as indicated by the opening lines of *My Native Land*:

> In Devonshire, my dearest home, I took my first repose,
> Ofttimes in my boyhood I've plucked the early rose;
> Walked in those handsome groves, lovely to be seen,
> Plucked those beautiful flowers, yellow, white and green.

Gay was married at Bratton on August 27, 1833, to Elizabeth Stanlake by Pastor Gurney. Mrs. Gay had been born July 1, 1807. His one love poem extant is *Coming Through the Rye*. Because this is found only in the 1883 volume, one might conclude that it referred to an event of his visit to England in 1882. But as the poet was then seventy-two years of age, it is more likely that the time recently spent amid the scenes of his youthful experiences recalled the happy hours of his courtship.

COMING THROUGH THE RYE

Our lives are swiftly passing,
The evening drawing nigh,
My dear and lovely lassie
Let us walk through this field of rye,
Spend many happy hours in it,
Kiss, shake hands good bye.

I looked on my lassie dear
With her beautiful black eyes.
I can never forget that night,
We spent among the rye;
Then lassie, when we meet again,
Pray do not act so shy.

O, my dear, we have met again,
The sun is shining high—
Once more, my loving lassie
To walk through the rye.
The time well spent, need not repent,
Kiss again, bye-bye.

Being again our fourth meeting
May it be to us a heavenly greeting,
And talk of the walks,
In the fields of the rye,
Often kissed each other,
Shake hands bye and bye.

Our walks together, do not lament,
Heaven is ours if we repent.

Emigrating to Canada with his bride in 1834, Gay settled in the town of Guelph, Upper Canada (now Ontario), and supported himself by carpentry, and ran a wagon shop. In a letter written in old age we find the remark: "I raised four of a family, who are a credit to me," from which we assume that his domestic life was full, satisfactory and normal. Mrs. Gay died on January 14, 1883.

From the age of twenty-four, through many years of patient industry, he plied his trade successfully, and on his own statement "amassed considerable money." In later life, he was established for a long time as a gunsmith and saw-filer, with a shop on the Market Square in Guelph. At different times he kept three hotels in Guelph, and nowhere is the quality of his seership more clearly illustrated than in his attitude toward liquor, a subject on which he might easily have become fanatical, as witness the Carrie Nation-like abandon of the lines:

> Let temperance be our guide while on this earth we stay;
> With good of all kinds
> Be on our minds,
> And throw all our grog bottles away,
> Like J. Gay.

But, perhaps from wisdom gained by his actual experience behind the bar, he elsewhere is more tolerant, and seems to distinguish between temperance and total abstinence. This position is defined in his poem *Temperance*:

Intemperance is the forerunner of crimes,
Draws thousands into rascality and death before their times;
And still don't blame liquor for all,
Other things too are not for the best;
We should never fill our bodies to excess.

More clearly still is his attitude on strong drink revealed in *The Great Exhibition*, composed for the occasion of a fair held in Guelph on September 2, 1875:

Other things came fresh to mind where on my bed I lays,
Of this great show which must take place
For four successive days.

Few words for our Town Innkeepers, I hope you won't get tight,
Carry out your business decently from morning until night,
So as our visitors by the thousands will return and have to say
They've been treated in our town of Guelph in a kind and
    friendly way.

This reminds us of another gainful occupation tried by Gay. He exhibited a two-headed colt at the Ontario fall fairs, and as a side-line sold cheap copies of his poems. The admission to see the deformed colt was ten cents, the price of the poems five. No record has been kept of what circulation the poems attained by this novel sales method; and the only known copies of these broadsheets or leaflets are now in the possession of the poet's grandson, William Teale. Many other authors have written their own advertisements, but Gay's is unique in the felicitous way that great art is put to strictly commercial use. It will be seen at a

glance that the prosody of the following announcement
is fully equal to that achieved by the poet when treating
so-called "exalted" themes, like *What is Man?* The
passage in question occurs as a lyric inset among the
plangent lines of *The Great Exhibition*:

> The greatest wonder for four days
> To be seen at the stall of the poet Gay's,
> His twoheaded Colt so tall and thin,
> The greatest sight that ever was seen.
>
> Come one, come all, as well you may,
> Ten cents will only be the pay,
> Gay's five-cent poems will all surprise,
> Both farmers and their loving wives.
>
> Then rally, strangers, from day to day,
> To hear the flute the poet play,
> Come forward, gents, both stout and tall,
> As fifteen cents will pay for all.

This flute is often mentioned by the poet, and is
now the property of William Teale. It is shown in the
fine portrait reproduced in the English edition of
the poems. The flute is an instrument that responds
to a wide range of moods. Schopenhauer, the pessimis-
tic philosopher, used his to soothe his sorrows. Gay
also suffered reverses, but affirms his happiness so often
that his flute must have vibrated to many a lively air.

To another James—Charles Canniff James, C.M.G.,
F.R.S.C., LL.D. (1863-1916)—who took a great interest
in Canadian literature, and published a *Bibliography*

of Canadian Poetry in 1899, we are indebted for a slight bit of portraiture. This occurs in a letter written by C. C. James on November 28, 1900, to Lawrence J. Burpee, F.R.G.S., F.R.S.C. Though the mention is regrettably lacking in detail, it is wórth quoting since we have so few records of Gay by his personal acquaintances.

DEAR MR. BURPEE,

I have seen your article on James Gay—"Jimmie Gay." Many a time he has trudged out to my laboratory at the Agricultural College, Guelph, with his little box containing flute and sheets of poems. He always spoke in rhyme, his rhyme: "Nice day—good day—James Gay—here today—soon away," etc. Then he would get up and recite one of his poems or make an impromptu speech in rhyme. By trade an umbrella-mender, saw-sharpener, Etc.

Yours &c.,

C. C. JAMES.

As we have seen, Gay sensibly avoided the pecuniary hardships that many other poets of marked ability have experienced before they won fame and a competence, yet his prudence did not save him from disaster; and it was through his simple trustfulness—typical of the poet's soul in him—that the tragedy occurred. Fancy him, decade after decade, starving his cravings to practice his art without interruption, but, instead, manfully caring for his family, and shrewdly saving his surplus earnings to provide for his old age; and realize the stark pathos of his misfortune: "I went security for our Tax Collector, who came behind in his funds which ruined me."¹

James Millington, the English critic, with whom Gay had some correspondence, was of the opinion that this calamity overtook the poet when he was keeping one of the hotels; and, in the absence of dates, the most reliable conjecture seems to be that the money accumulated as a carpenter and wagon-maker was invested in the succession of hotels, and after his loss Gay turned to the colt as a makeshift, finally settling down to his gun-smithing and saw-filing.

Possibly the colt period was also the time of his employment by Billy Hearn. As it is a difficult point to settle, I quote in full the Hearn poem, *Home Again*. It purports to have been written immediately on his arrival in Guelph after his trip to England in 1882; but as this was within the time of the Market Square shop, it seems likely that the Hearn illustration was drawn from his earlier life; and his obvious poverty at the time of the episode leads one to believe this hardship an aftermath of the faithless tax-collector incident.

HOME AGAIN

Home again as smart as ever,
Trusting in Christ the only giver,
Both on earth and in heaven forever.

If I could have seen what I had to go through,¹
I would have stuck to my home, believe me true,
They say we are never too old to learn,
This I found out from Billy Hearn.

I waited on this gentleman, night and day,
Received two shillings for my pay,
For feeding his cattle four times a day.

Truth is truth, I am sorry to say,
Hearn's cattle were better fed than Gay,
Far more, only he could not feed on hay.

In the absence of dates for the three hotel ventures several other hypotheses are possible. For instance, it is possible that the cattle-feeding episode followed his visit to England in 1860, which may have been financed out of the earnings of one of the hotels.

The poet's kindly disposition endeared him to all who had the privilege of knowing him. Natives of Guelph, who retain youthful memories of the celebrity in his later days, agree that he was a general favourite with the townspeople. Mr. H. J. B. Leadlay, present City Clerk, recalls that Mr. Harry P. Dill, United States Consul, took a keen interest in Gay's artistic endeavors, and went so far as to bear the cost of the publication of his poems. This would be the blue paper volume of 1883, published at Guelph under the title: *Poems by James Gay: Written While Crossing the Sea in 1882.*

The only record of his stay in Belleville, Ontario,

---

[1]Refers to his uncomfortable ocean passage, made miserable by the sailors "cursing and swearing all the way":—

Those sailors who came on board were a hard looking lot,
Cursing and swearing they had not forgot,
  No fear of death before their eyes,
  All but taken by surprise—
This is the life of the sailors on the sea.

suggests that he was equally popular there. The following is an undated clipping from the Belleville *Intelligencer* congratulating Gay upon his receipt of a medal:

> This is great news, and will be received with much satisfaction in this city, where the honoured poet condescended to reside for a time. We venture humbly to congratulate the new Laureate, whose verse is so much superior to that of G. W. Childs, A.M., of Philadelphia—the great mortuary poet of the age.

Gay said that he visited his native land after he had spent twenty-six years in Canada; that is, in 1860. Perhaps he was a year out in his count. Otherwise, it was a very long visit, as on the day of Prince Albert's death, December 14, 1861, Gay was in Plymouth, where an actual incident inspired the following memorial poem, which the poet modestly called "touching verses." Readers may think it strange that the "beast" is not described more fully. And assuredly it is strange that the author even neglects to name the species to which it belonged. This vagueness, which must be admitted to be a defect, may have been due to the poet's small stature having prevented him from seeing the animal over the heads of the crowd. If so, the creative imagination triumphed over the physical limitation.

A NOBLE MAN

In Plymouth town of high renown
There hung for public view
A beast well fed by our noble Prince;
Behold me this was true.

It hung in the street for quite a while, where thousands took
    their sight
A few days before this bright man his spirit took its flight.
        Our noble Prince he caused no strife,
        Taken away in prime of life;
        Taken from his partner and children dear,
        From them suddenly to disappear.
        All through his life was a kind-hearted man,
        Till death laid on him his chilly hand;
        With his partner lived for many a year,
        A loving parent and husband dear.
Our honoured Queen and Albert lived as patterns to old
    England and Scotland.
        To look at their children, though parted wide,
        Their mother's love is all their pride.
        Our Princess Louise could not take ease,
        To visit her mother across the seas.
        This has been a happy meeting,
        Return to her husband a happy greeting;
May that happy pair be spared for many a long day,
Until called to their homes where nothing never fades away.

In 1882, as previously mentioned, Gay again visited England, and on this occasion called at Queen Victoria's London residence to pay his homage; but she had left for Balmoral in Aberdeenshire, "so by me she was not seen." Since we have Gillis's graphic account of the interview that royal lady granted to Angus MacAskill, it is a pity that Gay did not gain audience. One can only wonder, in a mental hush, what effect these two great persons, with their strong and diverse natures, would have had on one another. In depriving the world of a portrait of Victoria by Gay, Fate was unkind.

Gay, however, addressed Her Majesty in several poems, and I am credibly informed that she wrote him letters of acknowledgment, which until recently were prized possessions of the poet's descendants, but have now been removed from their frames, and cannot be located at present.

Gay said: "I have been composing poetry all my life," and as so little of it can now be found it is likely that the bulk of his work, like Sappho's, has been lost. Even of that we cannot be sure. The only certainties are that one book of his verse was published in Guelph in 1883, and another from the Leadenhall Press, London, England, in 1884 or 1885. In the dedication to Tennyson, Gay speaks of himself as "nigh unto seventy-four." It is likely the birthday—March 24, 1884 —was reached between the penning of the immortal dedication and the date of publication; and there is strong reason for believing that the work was delayed in the press, and was not actually issued till 1885.

Publication was the culmination of one of the strangest romances of authorship. Many of Gay's poems, like *Welcome to Our Dominion* (to the Marquis of Lorne and H.R.H. Princess Louise) and *An Address to President Garfield,* were so obviously of a public nature that they must have been circulated. Some, we know, were given currency through various Canadian newspapers. As a result, there was some interest created in the United States, and a laudatory article on Gay's poetry appeared in the Detroit *Free Press*. Seeing this appreciation, a member of the firm of Field & Tuer wrote the poet: "Send us a volume of your poems and we will remit," expecting a printed copy of a moderately priced book. The poet understood the message as an offer to publish, and sent a book manuscript. On realizing the unique quality of the material, the English firm was ready to undertake the responsibilities of publication, and forthwith paid Gay £25 for his manuscript and publication rights.

The book, coming so late in the poet's life, did not give him much chance to win a wide public on this side of the Atlantic before his death on February 23, 1891, at Guelph, where he is buried in St. George's Woodlawn Cemetery. But during the last forty years a wide and keen interest has been taken in his work, to the extent that nearly all literary persons in the Dominion are familiar with at least some of his lines. Copies of the first edition get rarer as enquiries grow more frequent; and a second edition is badly needed. If one is brought out, it is to be hoped that the text of the 1883 book, none of which is duplicated in the better known English book, will be incorporated, and that the touching dedicatory epistle to Tennyson will be retained. Deep called to deep. No other composition conveys as succinctly the fine, unassuming spirit of the man (as in placing Longfellow above himself in merit), nor adumbrates so accurately the scope of the poet's creative labours.

To Dr. C. L. Alfred Tennyson,
    Poet Laureate of England, Baron, &c., &c.

Dear Sir,

Now Longfellow is gone there are only two of us left. There ought to be no rivalry between us two.

> "A poet's mind is clear and bright,
> No room for hatred, malice or spite."

To my brother poet, I affectionately dedicate these original verses not before printed. Other verses from my pen, when so inspired, have been numerously printed in Canadian and American papers:

> "Giving a few outlines of my fellow-man,
> As nigh as I can see or understand."

Almost the first poetry I can remember is the beautiful line—

> "Satan finds some mischief still for idle hands to do;"

and similar sentiments likewise occur in my own poems—

> "Up, up with your flag, let it wave where it will:
> A natural born poet his mind can't keep still."

I do not know whether a Baron or a Poet Laureate gets any wages in England. In Canada there is no pay.

> "Ambition is a great thing, of this I must say;
> This has been proved by the poet James Gay;
> He feels like Lord Beaconsfield, and best left alone;
> Respects every man and yet cares for none."

36

It is a solemn thing to reflect that I am the link connecting two great countries.

I hope when I am gone another may raise up.

I believe you have one boy, dear Sir, and I read in the papers the other day as he had been play-acting somewheres. I once exhibited a two-headed colt myself at several fairs, ten cents admission, and know something about play-acting and the like.

DON'T YOU LET HIM.

I hope to be in England sometime during the present year, if spared, and shall not fail to call round, if not too far from my lodging for a man nigh upon seventy-four, which, dear Sir, is the age of

Yours alway,

JAMES GAY,

(this day).

Poet Laureate of Canada
   and Master of All Poets.
Royal City of Guelph, Ontario.

II.—HIS POEMS

This world is round as a ball,
Some grow stout, others tall.
Some are born with talents bright,
Doing good from morn till night
Some for honesty, some for disgrace,
Thus you can see it in their face.

IN CONSIDERING THE POEMS THEMSELVES, THERE IS LITTLE use discussing their form. Either one accepts it, or one does not. Argument gets one nowhere: if a reader cannot feel the strength and beauty of these spontaneous utterances, he should stick to Milton and Pope and content himself outside the domain of modern art expression. I have no defence for Gay in his breach with tradition, beyond saying bluntly that he needs none. I fully realize that some people may not care for his poems: the loss is entirely theirs; and, further, I am bold enough to say that the very irregularities that Gay's detractors find annoying are the chief reason his poems are treasured by those who know how to appreciate them.

Having disposed thus of all questions of rhyme, rhythm, meter and tune pattern, we may enter at once upon the serious problems of intellectual content. At the outset one must remember that Gay—for all his rebelliousness in other matters—was pure Victorian in his belief that art is the handmaiden of morality, and the poet necessarily a preacher—by virtue of his calling better than other men. Hence his line in the poem on Guiteau, the murderer of President Garfield:

No man can compose aright when he is made captive by the devil.

Hence, too, the passage in his *Second Address to His Excellency the Marquis of Lorne and Her Royal Highness Princess Louise,* which might seem vain boasting in a lesser man, but is justified from one like Gay, who was conscious of a great message that must be delivered:

I hope to cross the seas and let Old England know it,
And to see Her Majesty in her own home, being the Master of all Poets.
As the greatest of Poets[1] have passed away,
It appears it's left between Alfred Tennyson and James Gay.

The altruistic aim is clearly shown in the rhymed prefatory note to the volume, which set a style, since occasionally followed, of printing verses in the form of prose. The concluding line is, to me, the most poignant of all the poet wrote; for here is the conscious artist secure in nothing but the knowledge of his own power: experienced in adversity, he knew that whatever ills he might still have to suffer, no one could prevent him from being a poet to his dying day.

---

[1]Longfellow.

CANADA'S POET

These poems composed are as nigh as I can, a truthful guide
For our fellow-man; composed by the Master of Poets,
James Gay, never to draw man's mind astray. Whoever buys my
Book, all should understand, those bright gifts received are not to
Be buried in sand. I am getting into years, I cannot walk so fleet;
Ofttimes I compose when walking on the street. Those gifts are
Great, I feel happy to say; no one on this earth can take this
Away.

Altruistic aims are found on every page. Not once
did he ever suggest that people should be guided by
base motives. Consistently, he promulgated the highest
ideals. This is so constant a factor in his writings that
one couplet from *November the First* is sufficient
illustration:

Leave off this sinful life and try to act more clever,
Put your trust in Providence, life changes like the weather.

It is therefore natural to find that Gay, broad and
tolerant in his theological views, was a religious man in
every sense. Seldom, however, has any ecclesiastical or
lay writer made such an impassioned defence of the
historical authenticity of the Old Testament as we find
in his *Samson*. The composition is doubly interesting.
Without this record later generations might never have
known how the Biblical strong man was once impugned,
since Gay did his work so thoroughly that after publication of his *Samson*, atheists never questioned the reality

of his story again, but concentrated their unbelief upon Jonah. And, in using again, with even greater mastery, the rhymed prose form, Gay exhausted its possibilities and never employed it in subsequent flights.

A FEW REMARKS ON SAMSON

It appears in his day he was both strong and fast, he killed Thousands of the Philistines with the jawbone of an ass. No such Man, we are well sure, ever lived on earth before. His wife Betrayed him in a cruel way, caused his death without delay. His Strength returned before too late; hundreds of his persecutors Received their just fate. His faith was very great at the last; he Killed more with himself than by the bone of the ass. Infidels Say this is all a farce, Samson never killed his enemies with the Jawbone of the ass. All those sayings spring by chance, just like Paris, the city of France.

Gay's humanitarianism is manifest often outside his assurances that all he writes is for the benefit of his fellow-man. It is seen in the homeliness of many lines, with their intimate personal touches and avoidance of the pretentious and ceremonial. In his memorial poem to the Guelph General Hospital, for instance, the great doctors get no mention, nor do the shining instruments of the operating room impress the poet; but instead the kindness of two women is enshrined eternally—Miss Giddis, who came to play to the patients on the organ, and Miss Hall who came weekly to read to them in a voice "loud and clear." So, too, when inspired to write upon the unfortunate Queen Mary of Scotland,

41

he does not dwell upon the jewelled crown she lost, nor even upon that more glorious crown of auburn tresses that was tragically removed by Elizabeth's axe-man, but he is touched rather by the pathos of a piece of fancywork representing who knows what anguish of heart in weary hours of solitude. It is the woman, not the queen, whom he would honour:

MARY QUEEN OF SCOTS

O Mary, Mary, Queen of Scot,
Your needlework is not forgot;
Three hundred years have passed, they say,
Your beautiful piece of tapestry is still in the hands of Mrs.
     Thomas Dunn, of Nassagaway.

This tenderness became a passion for peace. In the concluding passages from *Welcome to Our Dominion* quoted below, we again find that delightful informality to royalty resulting from seeing the individual before his exalted station:

Leave off party feeling as it's not becoming man,
And live as brothers ought to live on our Canadian land;
Live together without malice or strife,
Like our Governor and his beloved wife.[1]

His prejudice against the Jews is quite inconsistent, and can only be accounted for in the light of the intolerance that the Christianity of his day had established as a religious virtue.

---

[1] The Marquis of Lorne and H.R.H. Princess Louise.

ON THE JEWISH RACE

The Jews are still a spotted race.
Their manners are all times out of place:
Cannot live happy on this land,
Money always at their command.

Nothing prosperous to their views,
Always miserable are those Jews.
Nothing pleasing, nothing funny,
Always grasping after money.

No fear of God before their eyes,
No pleasure on earth,
No heaven when they die.
None but true christians raise on high.

In his day political rivalries were both more heated
than in ours on the part of the leaders, and were taken
more seriously by the common voter. Hence Gay's
aversion to party, illustrated in the selection on a
previous page quoted from *Welcome to Our Dominion,*
and which intensified until he made his famous
comparison between the poet and the politician that
remains unique in poetry:

POETRY AND POLITICS

Poetry and politics, believe in me,
It's impossible for both to agree;
A poet must be of a sound mind, and a man of a sound
Principle, his gifts received are of the best,
No taste for politics, whatever, why he cannot take his rest.
A political man will stand and argue with his opponent from
    morning till night;
Where this is carried out is malice and spite;
The best politics ever man possessed,
Are truth and honesty, and his mind at rest.

THE FOUR JAMESES

A poet's mind is clear and bright,
No room for hatred, malice or spite;
All through the day he is pleasant and kind,
Nothing doubtful on his mind;
His mind made up, he can't keep still,
From doing what is right as well.
The political man can do his best,
And still his mind is not at rest;
If we want to gain poetical treasure,
We must leave off sin and earthly pleasure;
Cast pride and spite away;
Live happy like your poet, James Gay.

It was natural that, holding such a philosophy, Gay should live according to its dictates, and, doing so, become an optimist.

ALL IS WELL

This is a great thing, I must say:
When the mind is right we should have peace every day.
May we all keep in our right minds,
Will be a happy thing to tell;
We can then go on rejoicing all is well, all is well.

James Gay will be your guide from cradle to the grave;
Then why go against his will, and act the cunning knave?
Guard against the wicked man, he soon will take to flight;
Be on our guard each day we live, we shall find ourselves
    all right.

We have this watchword on the sea,
Where mariners all they should agree:
"Who goes there? Stranger, quickly tell."
"Friend, all is well, all is well."

44

This should be the password on land,
On a dark night it would be a good plan.
If this be carried out all through,
Our life will be a pleasant tale to tell,
When lying on our beds unwell, all is well, all is well.

The last line marks the complete triumph of mind over matter.

By peace, Gay meant domestic peace; for he was a fervent patriot, and evidently regarded the doctrine of internationalism as immorally flabby. The clearest statement of his loyalty occurs in his *Address to His Excellency the Marquis of Lorne and Her Royal Highness Princess Louise,* which ends with the stirring lines:

England, with all her faults, I love her still,
Let men of no principle say what they will;
There are thousands of rotten Engishmen, I must confess,
Turn their back on their country and dirt their nest.
For my Queen and my country I've always proved true,
And my colours will stand by the Red, White, and Blue.

Nor had imperialism ever a more trustful disciple. Its essence was "the white man's burden," the unquestioning belief that British arms were always the obvious instrument of the Almighty to bring weaker races to repentance. Kipling, at his most bombastic, never expressed this pure faith with greater clarity or force than did Gay in his public espousal of the British cause in Egypt:

WHAT ABOUT THIS EGYPTIAN AFFAIR?

It seems they are a wicked race,
The British flag they don't embrace;
I hope old England will come out right,
So as those wicked heathens will have no sight;
Murdering the innocent every day,
I hope before long will receive their pay.
No fear of death before their eyes,
Let's hope John Bull will take them by surprise,
Meet them fairly face to face:
Brave Englishmen will overcome this savage race;
Mr. General Sir Garnet is in the field,
All wicked men to him will have to yield;
They will do their best to carry the sway,
But England at last will gain the day;
Then, Rule, Britannia, Britannia rules the waves,
And by the help of Mr. Sir Garnet will show those Egyptians
    their silent graves;
No rascality or cruelty can prosper wherever it's carried out,
So those rascals by thousands will disappear before they know
    what they are about.
Let us all do what we can
For the good and prosperity of our fellow-man.

To the thoughtless, the final couplet may seem to contain an incongruous sentiment, and to have been hitched on merely to wind off in a good moral tone. Actually, it is the logical conclusion of the whole diatribe, and sets down more starkly than any other words ever penned the heart of later Victorian imperialism, which had become a religion—a creed as austere, simple and hard as Mahommedanism. The poem has its roughnesses; but it has passion, sincerity, and its own fierce

46

logic. By not embracing the British flag, the Egyptians proved themselves wicked; and as they were so recalcitrant as to offer active resistance, there was nothing to be done in their own best interests but to slaughter them. Being heathens, the sooner they were dispatched the better. Thus the phrase about "the good and prosperity of our fellow-man" is neither cant nor an irrelevancy, but the praise of war waged for purely altruistic purposes.

When considering events nearer home, Gay's patriotism was less sanguinary. On first surveying the Canadian scene the weather seems to be the only rebellious factor. As he broods, however, he perceives that subtle disturber of the peace, the "wicked spirit" of the poem, that dominates the latter half of it. Though without the dignity of capitals, he is, of course, Satan, the Eternal Troubler, who also dominated *Paradise Lost* to the extent of becoming the real hero of that drama. This explanation anticipates, and I hope disposes of, the charge of irrelevancy that might be made by the hasty reader. Gay is not irrelevant. Like Browning, he leaps from concept to concept without recording each intermediate step in his reasoning; and the lazy-minded sometimes fail to follow him in what are not, after all, very tortuous processes of thought. His utterance is always cryptic, his thought always logical. This poem passes from the changeableness of the weather, through the changeableness of man's mind and the diabolic cause of human unrest, to the frightful reward of wickedness. In the original printing the lines follow closely. I have taken the liberty of breaking them into stanzas to bring out the meaning more clearly; and, as they fall into four four-line groups, I believe I am restoring the poem to the form Gay designed.

CANADIAN CLIMATE

Canadian climate must have been changeable ever since the world
     begun,
One hour snowing, and the next raining like fun,
Our blood sometimes thick, other times thin,
This is the time colds begin.

After all, people seem strong and healthy;
Some die poor, others wealthy:
So men's minds are like the weather,
Cannot agree very long together.

This wicked spirit is around every day
To keep the minds of man astray;
The rich man's mind he does unfold,
And tells him how to make his gold;

No fear of death before his eyes,
Often taken by surprise.
O! What will be the rich man's fate?
Too late! too late, too late.

The gnomic quality of those verses is certainly reminiscent of some of William Blake's. They are quoted, however, to show the milder nature of Gay's feelings of patriotism within Canada's borders. When it is a matter of civic pride, and he is extolling his beloved city, not even the Devil can disturb the transquility of his love:

You travel east, you travel west, return to Guelph and say it's best.

While I deny the validity of all criticisms aimed at the alleged lack of logical sequence in Gay's lines, I admit unhesitatingly the poet's marked originality. It is his chief distinguishing characteristic. He is the least derivative of all poets. No one ever wrote like him before; and he has never been successfully imitated.

Of this originality he must have been quite aware; for when he wrote *The Elephant and the Flea* which is generally considered his masterpiece, he prefaced the poem with a note explaining that he had hit upon a theme never before treated poetically. Gay's effort is entirely satisfying; and it is safe to predict that no future poet will have the courage to attempt anything on the same subject. It stands—without predecessor or successor—unique and triumphant:

THE ELEPHANT AND THE FLEA

Between those two there's a great contrast,
The elephant is slow, the flea very fast,
You can make friends with the elephant and gain his good-will,
If you have a flea in your bed you cannot lie still:
A flea is a small thing, all times in the way,
Hopping and jumping like beasts after their prey,

Oft dropt inside your ears—don't think this a wonder,
You will think for a while it's loud claps of thunder:
We can make friends with all beasts ever came in our way—
No man on earth can make friends with a flea;
The elephant is a large beast, and cunning no doubt;
If you offend him, look out for his snout;
Give him tobacco, it will make him ugly and cross,
A blow from his trunk's worse than a kick from a horse;
And still they are friendly, will cause no disaster,
Beg around in shows, make money for their master:
On this noble beast, the elephant, I have no more to say;
And this little black insect will have its own way.
A flea you may flatten if you know how,
But an elephant no man can't serve so anyhow.
One thing seems wonderful to your poet, James Gay—
All beasts and little animals seem to have a cunning way;
Just like the whales at sea, they seem to know their foes,
Upsets their boats in a moment, and down they goes.

There only remains to be said that besides being an ideal mirror of his own times, the poet fulfilled that other high function of the bard — prevision. The following stanza from *The Great Exhibition* contains his marvellously accurate prophecy of the present agrarian movement:

It's by the plough the farmer thrives,
And keeps poor men happy with their wives;
Through him, too, may well be said,
That little children receive their bread.
In fact we need not frown or brawl, the honest farmer pays for
    all.

It was not till thirty years after that was written that the farmers' bloc was formed in the United States and the farmers' parties, when formed, began immediately to play a leading part in Canadian politics. Yet Gay, with his sharpened intuition, had laid his hand on the mainspring of the whole movement: "the honest farmer *pays for all*." That exploitation of the unorganized agriculturist was the seat of the whole trouble, and led in time to the extensive and powerful farmers' organizations of the present, which ensure the food producer against paying any more than his share. Possibly much less.

James Gay was a dear old man. His inspiration is undeniable. He expressed the beliefs and prejudices of his day in terse, idiomatic Canadian. The bluntness of his diction precluded high polish; but it is flint-like in solidity. His vanity was all on the surface: at heart he was simple as a child, and the soul of humility. Above all, he was that rare and fine creature, a man with a mind of his own. Well has he earned his coveted peace eternal in that bright land where, in his own words, "nothing never fades away."

51

James McIntyre: The Cheese Poet

I.—COWS AND COFFINS

Scotsmen have wandered far and wide
From Moray Frith to Frith of Clyde,
McDonald from his sea girt isle,
And Campbell from his broad Argyle.

Here to-night in this array
Is Murray, McKenzie and McKay,
And there doth around us stand
The Munroe, Ross and Sutherland.

IN THE LITTLE VILLAGE OF FORRES, MORAYSHIRE, Scotland, made forever famous by Macbeth's slaying of King Duncan, which Shakespeare was later to immortalize in the most popular of his tragedies, two men were born in houses exactly opposite each other, in the early part of the nineteenth century. Both of them were to play significant parts in the upbuilding of the Dominion of Canada, that was not to come into federated existence for another forty years. The elder, born in 1820, was Donald Alexander Smith, who, at the time of his death in 1914 was Baron Strathcona and Mount Royal, having been Governor of the Hudson's Bay Company, President of the Bank of Montreal, a

Privy Councillor, Canadian High Commissioner in London, and one of the small group of Canadian financiers to whom we owe the Canadian Pacific Railway. The younger, the subject of this study, was James McIntyre, born in 1827, whose contribution to the land of his adoption was in the realm of poetry; and at his death in 1906, he wore proudly the title, casually but affectionately and irrevocably bestowed on him, of the Cheese Poet.

The connection between these men went further than the mere accident of birth. We must believe that the two boys, being neighbors, were also friends; and that the younger would be greatly influenced by the elder. We can imagine Smith, as a lad of eighteen, before his departure for North America in 1838 in the service of the Hudson's Bay Company, firing the lively imagination of his eleven-year-old chum with tales of anticipated adventure and advancement in the semi-mythical British American Colonies, where under the Constitutional Act of 1791 the names Upper Canada and Lower Canada (now Ontario and Quebec) were already in use. So it was the most natural thing that in 1841, when young McIntyre was fourteen—a time boys often left home in those days—he should have followed Smith's example and migrated to a land of opportunity that had already absorbed his friend three years earlier. It is not only possible, but likely, that

young Smith's letters home directly encouraged McIntyre to migrate; for Smith was successful from the
first, and would have picturesque tales to tell of his life
at a Labrador "post"; and as he was always a man to
see opportunity well in advance of others, he must have
felt then the same optimism that led him later to risk
his all in the Canadian Pacific Railway venture, after
English engineers had failed, and when English financiers declared the scheme the height of folly as a
business undertaking.

It is interesting, too, to learn that in the later period
of their lives, when Lord Strathcona was a millionaire
and James McIntyre a much-admired poet, the latter
composed a poem upon the Strathcona Horse regiment,
that the fiancier had equipped for service in South
Africa; and Strathcona was so pleased with it that he
sent its author $100. That does not seem a great sum
now; but to a Canadian poet in the lean year 1899
it represented munificence, and McIntyre was deeply
touched and very grateful for the much needed assis-
tance.

Unfortunately, insufficient records have been kept
of the poet's early life; and so we cannot say whether
McIntyre came to Canada on Smith's specific invitation, or whether the older boy met the younger, or
arranged an opening for him. What is known definitely
is that, like other early citizens we admire, he had to

struggle for his foothold in a land that still was rough
and largely unsettled. When past sixty he wrote:

> Our first Canadian job when boy,
> In the big woods we did enjoy,
> Large maple bush we then did tap
> And to camp carried maple sap.
>
> We stored it in great wooden trough,
> Then in big kettles sugared off,
> Though often it did try our mettle
> To keep up fire beneath each kettle.
>
> Of old we thought our neck was broke
> By having on it a neckyoke,
> And on each side a heavy pail
> Suspended from the yoke by bail.
>
> We waded through the snow and slush
> And stumbled o'er the logs in bush,
> But no doubt the maple's sweeter
> Than any other thing in meter.
>
> Let none at sugar making scoff
> Webster was rocked in a sap trough;
> When boiling sap it is quite handy
> To pour some in snow to make candy.

It was hard work but it had its compensations. The
carrying of two full buckets of sap through the treach-
erous melting snow of the spring woods was no joke,
especially for a boy of fourteen, and young McIntyre
must have had good stuff in him. The next glimpse we
get of him is about a month later, when the farmer
set him to work to burn down the trees, as the custom
then was. The poem describing this is not quoted in

full. The point of the narrative is that the "withered pine" nearly burned down the house and barn also, and the lad, who was alone, had a strenuous, but victorious, battle with the flames. The incident is so typical of the wanton destruction of the valuable forests of Southern Ontario at that time, that I quote rather more than enough to fix the nature of its author's then occupation:

LAND CLEARING

The first winter which I did spend
In Canada was with a friend,
And when the snow had passed away
Quite early in the month of May,

Friend started off for a barn raising,
And told me to get stumps ablazing,
Around each stump I heaped a pile
Of roots and junks of wood so vile.

For he wished the field to clear
So it a crop of roots would rear,
And there was one high withered pine
Which was full of turpentine.

Fire started and with it a breeze
Carried the sparks 'mong leaves of trees,
I did work hard but for recompense
·All was saved but a few rails of fence.

Man in spring logging oft awakes
From winter slumbers nests of snakes,
And listens to the music grand
Of bull frogs, our Canadian band.

It is remarkable that at the same time this was written, Archibald Lampman was writing one of his distinctively Canadian masterpieces, *The Frogs,* and that both poets were moved to admiration of our so-friendly, cheerful and ubiquitous native reptile. As to the waste of timber, Peter McArthur lived to regret this bitterly. McIntyre, who died twenty years earlier, and whose great passion was for the produce of the farm—dairy products in chief—worked in wood, and soon realized the primitive folly of destroying walnut, oak and cherry trees.

We must assume that during the summer he remained on that unidentified farm, doing the chores, making hay, and serving his apprenticeship as many another young immigrant from the Old Country has done before and since. From this period also came the poem on *The Old Snake Fence,* a picturesque institution that has fallen before the efficiency of wire, for which one can work up no enthusiasm whatever. This poem begins:

> In early times the pioneer
> When a few acres he did clear,
> He found an ample recompense
> For splitting rails and making fence.
>
> Though it was crooked as a snake,
> And zigzag style did not awake,
> He thought it was a thing of beauty,
> Yet in its day it did its duty.

Well, I am proud to say I am sufficiently of the soil to think it "a thing of beauty", too, and to mourn its departure.

Now for some years we lose track of McIntyre altogether. At some period, which we have no means of fixing, he married Euphemia Fraser, by whom he had two children—a boy who died in 1876, and Kate McIntyre Ruttan, now a widow living at Lavallee, Ontario. There is, of course, a possibility that there is some grain of autobiographical truth in his long poem, *Canadian Romance:*

> An English youth to Canada came,
> A labourer, John Roe by name.
>
> *   *   *   *
>
> He added to his wealth each year
> For independence he loved dear,
> He knew a labourer he would be
> Forever in the old country,
> His forefathers had tilled the ground
> And never one had saved a pound.
> Their one luxury around their door
> A few choice flowers their garden bore,
> But never hoped to own the soil
> But serve as hinds to sweat and toil,
> To work and toil for him had charm
> He hoped some day to own a farm,
> So he hired with Reuben Tripp
> The wealthiest man in the township.
> Tripp's only child, his daughter Jane,—

The story goes on that the suit prospered, and John and Jane were married, and ultimately inherited father Tripp's farm. But what is more interesting in this narrative is the wonderfully faithful picture of pioneer life in old Ontario, quite Chaucerian in its care for details. From McIntyre's descriptions, these scenes could be painted as easily as could the portraits of the Canterbury pilgrims. There is something also in the terseness of the lines that reminds one of the famous *Prologue*, with which McIntyre may well have been familiar, since there is no doubt that he was widely read in the English poets. The young wife, Jane, is represented as helping her husband as actively as those pioneer women did help their men:

> She helped him in the fields to reap,
> And spun the wool from off the sheep,
> All they required they had for both,
> Of her own weaving of good cloth,
> And she was a good tailoress,
> Did make his coat and her own dress;

(If those last two couplets are not the very rhythm and rhyme of Chaucer, I do not know how else to define them.)

> The golden butter that she made
> Was of the very finest grade,
> She filled large pot with well knead dough
> And baked fine bread 'mong embers glow;

The poem then gives an equally full account of his labors, which included the felling of trees. The largest he could only weaken at the base by cutting rings

around them, and waiting for natural forces to complete
the work:

> For many a time the furious breeze
> Would quick o'erthrow the girdled trees,
> And sometimes they would kill the cows
> When they did feed on grass or browse.

Whether McIntyre himself married the daughter of
a well-to-do family, as this poem might suggest, or
whether he earned the necessary capital, we soon find
him doing business as a furniture dealer in St.
Catharines, whose merits he has extolled:

> St. Catharines famed for mineral waters
> And for the beauty of her daughters,
>
> *   *   *   *
>
> St. Catharines your greatness you inherit
> From the genius of a Merritt,
> You still would be a village dreary
> But for this canal from Lake Erie.
>
> Among its many great rewards
> It gives you dry docks and ship yards

*   *   *   *

I have been unable to learn the date of McIntyre's
removal to Ingersoll, which had such a profound effect
on his art. He there established a furniture factory on
the banks of the Thames, and in connection therewith
ran a furniture store, where he sold card tables, pianos,
beds, chairs, coffins, and caskets. As is still the case
in many of the smaller places in the Dominion, the

local furniture dealer was also the professional under-taker, or "mortician" as he would be called now. In this calling he prospered reasonably—as one who knew him puts it, "he was always able to pay his debts"— and was more than locally known through his con-nection with the Oxford County organization of the Liberal Party.

That the move had been made by 1859 we know from an anecdote McIntyre has related of Thomas D'Arcy McGee's visit to Ingersoll in that year. When McGee rose to speak, "the chair being new stuck to him", and the orator said he hoped the people of Montreal would be as anxious as the people of Inger-soll evidently were for him to retain his seat. McIntyre would perhaps be present in a dual capacity: McGee was then allied to the "Reformers", or Liberals, and the chair with the adhesive varnish was likely one of McIntyre's—rented for the evening.

The error in the date that is found in the prose note to the Gourlay poem seems to be only a slip of memory. Gourlay, "the first to agitate for popular rights in Canada" (1817-20), was impeached by the Family Compact, and banished. He returned to Canada only in 1856; and contested the Oxford seat in 1860, not in 1858 as McIntyre asserts. The poem is quoted here to show McIntyre's interest in politics, and because

Gourlay has been almost lost sight of as a Canadian political figure, and because of the striking simile, "like noble ruined castle wall."

ROBERT FLEMING GOURLAY

There came to Oxford Robert Gourlay,
In his old age his health was poorly;
He was a relic of the past,
In his dotage sinking fast;
Yet he was erect and tall
Like noble ruined castle wall.
In early times they did him impeach
For demanding right of speech,
Now Oxford he wished to represent
In Canadian parliament,
But him the riding did not honour,
But elected Doctor Connor.

At home, McIntyre's acquaintance was wide, since he was a zealous Mason, and a member of the Masonic Order for forty years, and for fifty years was a member of the Independent Order of Odd Fellows. In the lodges of both these societies he filled the highest positions with honor. Since funerals were often arranged by these orders, doubtless a good deal of business came to him through them. During the last twenty years of his life he enjoyed a wide reputation as a poet, the late Sir John S. Willison, who was prominent in the Liberal Party at the time, printing some of McIntyre's verses in the Toronto *Globe,* of which Sir John was then the distinguished editor.

But misfortune came to McIntyre when he took into partnership William Watterworth and Sam Crotty. The firm soon became bankrupt. This disaster was felt very keenly by McIntyre, who was reduced to such financial straights that, to use the language of his daughter, Mrs. Kate Ruttan, her father "couldn't pay for a sitting hen." It seems that even Nature conspired at this time to bring sorrow to her devoted son and eloquent mouthpiece; for in another communication —a telegram this time—Mrs. Ruttan, with characteristic impetuosity, tells of the destruction of her father's place of business by flood and fire:

HIS FACTORYS FOUNDATION FELL FROM THAMES TORRENT COFFINS CASKETS CARD TABLES PIANOS PIANOLOS BEDS BUNKS ETC SAILED DOWN RIVER THAMES WILL WRITE TONIGHT AWAIT MY LETTER BURNED UP FLOODED DOWN KATE RUTTAN

The fuller explanation in the letter runs:

He was the bright & shining star of Ingersoll Literary Society, attended a Night School for Elocution, & taught (unofficially), the boys, how to "spout." "Spout" was his own word for "declaiming or elocution or harangue." One morn at six he heard the crack of doom & the crash of worlds. His 3 story steam furniture factory fell, (note 3 f's) "Apt alliteration's artful aid." Foundation of furniture factory fell & sailed down the River Thames. Coffins, caskets, cupboards, card tables, chairs, pianos, pianolas—all commingled in confusion worse confounded. Also he was previously burned out. He wrote me his true townsmen collected Six Hundred Dollars for him that mournful morn. He was the loveliest man on earth.

63

It has been erroneously stated that McIntyre had a very large factory and business, and died wealthy. It is generally believed that he was in the cheese business, and some have even thought that it was his own factory that made the "Mammoth Cheese" that was sent to the World's Fair at Paris, and inspired the poem generally recognized as McIntyre's masterpiece.

There is not the slighest foundation of truth in any of these rumors. McIntyre was not basely advertising his own concern when he wrote his various lyrics in praise of milch cows and the dairy industry that caused Oxford to be called "the banner county of Ontario." Any one who has ever penetrated to the upper story of one of these combined furniture and undertaking establishments, and found it stocked with stains and varnishes and embalming fluids, and very likely a corpse stretched out on a bench awaiting treatment, will realize that it was no place for the making of cheeses; and that McIntyre, who had an eye to the fitness of things, did not deal in foodstuffs, except in verse. His trade has been defined once for all in the memorial poem by Kate Ruttan:

TO JAS. McINTYRE

An undertaker bold
Who can't be undersold,
    Jas. McIntyre;
He has caskets rich and rare,
Fit for the young and fair,
    All you'd desire.

And incomplete our verses,
Did we forget his hearses
    All built of glass,
And draped with hangings golden,
Of barbaric splendour olden,
    None can surpass.

His book he'll give you gratis,
Filled with divine afflatus
    And local news;
High on the wall of fame
He hath written out his name,
    Inscribed his muse.

McIntyre was genuinely inspired by the fertile and lovely mixed farming district around Ingersoll—as who is not moved that has ever seen that rich and beautiful country? And he was thrilled by the epic-pastoral drama of this large tract of Canada's loveliest land saved from ruin by excessive wheat raising through the introduction of cheese and butter making on a large scale. It was, in truth, a wonderful union—the grazing herds on the hill-side, the equivalent of the shepherd life the Greek poets sang of, with modern industrialism and international trade—so fruitful that it served to keep that portion of Ontario the garden one wishes it may always remain.

His poetic insight gave him early knowledge of all this; and if his themes are new, surely they are none the worse for that. There is plenty of precedent of the first order for a poet's endeavor to get away from sterile classicism, and refresh his art by singing of the heroic and beautiful in the life around him, even though the objects and thoughts he treats in his verse are so common as to be vulgarly thought prosaic. Instead of filling his landscapes with non-existent gods and goats and shepherdesses, he saw beauty in what was actually in every meadow—the pacific face of the cow:

THE VALE OF THAMES

In vale of Thames oft'times are seen
The cattle graze 'mong sweetest green,
Or there contented with their fate[1]
The gentle cows do ruminate.

And enjoy a double pleasure
In re-chewing hidden treasure,
The cow is a kindly creature,
Kind and pleasant in each feature.

So McIntyre found his avocation. He became the supreme voice of the dairy industry and of the prosperous and progressive farmers of Oxford County; who were almost as content with their fate as the cows themselves. His first volume, *Musings on the Banks of the Canadian Thames,* was published in 1884; and was followed in 1889 by the larger collected and definitive volume, *Poems of James McIntyre.* Both books were greatly in demand, and attained large circulations for that time. He was respected and beloved by all who knew him. Engaged with his

---

[1]Dairy cows would naturally be more contented with their fate than range cattle, that go to the slaughter-house at the age of one or two years.

lodges, a member of the Erskine Presbyterian Church, a shrewd man of business, honest and fair in all his dealings, selling card tables and pianos to the living and burying the dead, singing the cow from the beauty of her nose to the economic value of her manure, he graced the City of Ingersoll for many years, and died there at the age of seventy-nine, on March 5, 1906, greatly mourned as one who had been unfalteringly a public-spirited citizen.

II.—THE SONG OF ECONOMIC SALVATION

> Then let the farmers justly prize
> The cows for land they fertilize,
> And let us all with songs and glees
> Invoke success into the cheese.

JAMES MCINTYRE WAS LIVING IN INGERSOLL WHEN cheese-making began there, and he witnessed the triumphant expansion of the industry in the late seventies and eighties. Then it was that the farmers, exuberant over the new-found source of wealth, were at the pitch of their enthusiasm for the enterprise. Probably more cheese is now made in Ingersoll than McIntyre ever dreamed of—and he was bold in prophecy—but the inhabitants take it more prosaically. They are busier now in scientific merchandising than in trying to make monuments that, in their assault on the eye, may capture the imagination also, and impress the world with the jubilant news of their economic salvation. Then, however, in their delirious ecstasy, it was most natural that they should have endeavored to manufacture for display the largest cheese ever moulded by man; and history does not say they failed. This monster production weighed over seven thousand pounds. It doubtless accomplished the object of its makers; but it is doubtful whether it would have been widely remembered if it had not thrilled James McIntyre to the point of composing his immortal:

ODE ON THE MAMMOTH CHEESE

We have seen thee, queen of cheese
Lying quietly at your ease,
Gently fanned by evening breeze,
Thy fair form no flies dare seize.

All gaily dressed soon you'll go
To the great Provincial show,
To be admired by many a beau
In the city of Toronto.

Cows numerous as a swarm of bees,
Or as the leaves upon the trees,
It did require to make thee please,
And stand unrivalled, queen of cheese.

May you not receive a scar as
We have heard that Mr. Harris
Intends to send you off as far as
The great world's show at Paris.

Of the youth beware of these,
For some of them might rudely squeeze
And bite your cheek, then songs or glees
We could not sing, oh! queen of cheese.

We'rt thou suspended from balloon,
You'd cast a shade even at noon,
Folks would think it was the moon
About to fall and crush them soon.

This monstrous lump of edible matter was a constant inspiration to McIntyre, for his poet's eye rightly saw it as a symbol of the glory of his community; and in another poem he explains just why a big cheese represents virtues that a little cheese cannot:

> In barren district you may meet
> Small fertile spot doth grow fine wheat,
> There you may find the choicest fruits,
> And great, round, smooth and solid roots.
>
> But in conditions such as these
> You cannot make a mammoth cheese,
> Which will weigh eight thousand pounds,
> But where large fertile farms abounds.
>
> Big cheese is synonymous name,
> With fertile district of the Thame,
> Here dairy system's understood,
> And they are made both large and good.

The romance that underlay this development, that was perceived by the poet, and caused him to dedicate his pen to its expression, began with the wretched state of agriculture in that section about the middle of the nineteenth century. The forests had been wiped out; the land had been long tilled, and was suffering badly from unscientific over-production of wheat. The hopes of the pioneers seemed, for the time, to have been misplaced. The farmers were discouraged. Also, when matters were at their worst, disturbing rumors came back to them from those who had gone to the Canadian West.

> Ontario cannot compete
> With the Northwest in raising wheat,
> For cheaper there they it can grow
> So price in future may be low.

The problem was to find some cheap fertilizer for the depleted soil. Cheese offered the ideal solution. Canada then imported it in great quantities. A man by the name of Ranney, who "began with just two cows" in 1856, soon had a large herd, plenty of natural fertilizer, and a most valuable by-product in the cheese he made on his farm on the dairy plan. Ten years after Ranncy's start, Farrington in 1866, at the time plans for Confederation were in final shape, was the first to make this form of manufacturing his sole business, and thus spread the prosperity that had come to Ranney:

> The farmers they now all make rich
> Since Farrington went to Norwich,
> And the system first there began
> Of making cheese on factory plan;

This move revolutionized agriculture in that part of Ontario, and brought the farmers suddenly from despair to affluence. Soon they were exporting ten million dollars' worth of cheese annually; and it was their joy over this unexpected deluge of good fortune that communicated itself to McIntyre, and led him to

devote his finest talents to celebrating cheese. The
wealth he had perhaps visualized in his Scottish home
in the form of nuggets had come at last to his community in the form of round, golden cheeses. The
whole history of the movement, and its significance, is
epitomized in the *Oxford Cheese Ode*. Though there
is a sublimity in the lines on that single, gigantic cheese
that the *Oxford Ode* does not quite equal, the latter
unquestionably has an epic quality of spaciousness: in
structure it is much smoother, and it is one of
McIntyre's best poems:

OXFORD CHEESE ODE

The ancient poets ne'er did dream
That Canada was land of cream,
They ne'er imagined it could flow
In this cold land of ice and snow,
Where everything did solid freeze,
They ne'er hoped or looked for cheese.

A few years since our Oxford farms
Were nearly robbed of all their charms,
O'er cropped the weary land grew poor
And nearly barren as a moor,
But now their owners live at ease
Rejoicing in their crop of cheese.

And since they justly treat the soil,
Are well rewarded for their toil,
The land enriched by goodly cows
Yields plenty now to fill their mows,
Both wheat and barley, oats and peas,
But still their greatest boast is cheese.

And you must careful fill your mows
With good provender for your cows,
And in the winter keep them warm,
Protect them safe all time from harm,
For cows do dearly love their ease,
Which doth ensure best grade of cheese.

To us it is a glorious theme
To sing of milk and curds and cream,
Were it collected it could float
On its bosom, small steam boat,
Cows numerous as swarm of bees
Are milked in Oxford to make cheese.

A great deal of space is taken up with allied and subsidiary matters. There are poems to the pioneers, Ranney, Salford and Farrington; and every phase of the industry is discussed with expert knowledge. McIntyre must have immersed himself in cream, and made cheese his chief mental diet, for years. To the new gospel of dairying, he was a convert so ardent that he barely missed becoming fanatical. He is saved by the sound sense of his remarks, and Joaquin Miller was justified in telling him he did wisely in "singing of useful themes." Here, in *Lines Read at a Parsonage Opening at the Village where Ranney had once flourished, 1883,* we see the general benefit of the enterprise, whereas the last quoted poem focussed attention upon the revenues derived directly from the cheese. Notice, then, the indirect blessings:

The farmers are in cheerful mood,
For harvest all it has been good,
And all the grain was sown this spring
An abundant yield will bring.

And you can scarcely stow away
The yield of barley, oats and hay,
Such pasture it is seldom seen,
E'en now it is so fresh and green.

This beauteous colour nature decks,
While it insures you large milk cheques,
And certes you've much cause to praise,
For hogs and cattle that you raise.

The whole family profited as well as the farmer himself. To explain the quotation showing how their wives' happiness was increased by the advent of cheese, it should be stated that it has been a Canadian farm custom for the wives to treat the eggs and the butter they make as their personal incomes. These commodities are traded at the village store, and the women get in exchange whatever dress goods or groceries they need. The inauguration of cheese-making caused all dairy produce to go up in price.

And the ladies dress in silk
From the proceeds of the milk,
But those who buy their butter,
How dear it is, they mutter.

McIntyre's altruism is nowhere better illustrated than in his pleasure over enhanced prices of these things of which he was a consumer only. His sympathies were too much engaged for him to worry about his own small losses. Or perhaps the farmers now bought more and better furniture, and indulged in more expensive funerals. Be that as it may, he gives advice on the different breeds of cattle, and elaborate instructions for their care and feeding:

> If bran slops you on cow bestow
> Of milk it will increase the flow.

He tells of the proper seasons for making cheese, and when not to:

> Our muse it doth refuse to sing
> Of cheese made early in the spring,
> The quality is often vile
> Of cheese that is made in April.

Any sort of cheese his muse would balk at must have been reprehensible cheese indeed. But thus he goes on, even covering sanitation in the dairy:

> Utensils must be clean and sweet,
> So cheese with first class can compete,
> And daily polish up milk pans,
> Take pains with vats and milk cans.

Nor does he forget to put in a good word for his home town, to attract the business of the farmers, whose interests he had made his own:

> Now we close this glorious theme,
> This song of curds and rich cream,
> You can buy your hoops and screws,
> And all supplies for dairy use,
> Milk cans and vats, all things like these,
> In Ingersoll great mart for cheese,
> Here buyers all do congregate
> And pay for cheese the highest rate.

75

He was determined that, if possible, there shall be no waste in this dairy business; and therefore he was eager to turn all by-products to profitable use:

> Grant has here a famous work
> Devoted to the cure of pork,
> For dairymen find it doth pay
> To fatten pigs upon the whey,
> For there is money raising grease
> As well as in the making cheese.
>
> * * * *
>
> And it pays best to sell each pig,
> Plump and young, not old, fat and big,
> Young and tender now's the vogue
> Either in cattle or in hog.

And it was inevitable that he should occasionally step over into agricultural fields that have no connection at all with cheese:

> And in Ontario the hen
> Is worthy of the poet's pen,
> For she doth well deserve the praise
> Bestowed on her for her fine lays.

That is as far as we shall accompany the poet in his "glorious theme" *as such;* but it is impossible to promise it will not crop up again incidentally, for he is so in love with his pleasant faced cows that their sweet breath is smelled even in his definition of poetry:

> For poetry is the cream,
> And essence of the common theme.

What his lyric encouragement meant to the people of his community we can only guess. It is good to know, however, how fully his desires for their advancement have been fulfilled:

> All dairymen their highest aims
> Should be to make the vale of Thames,
> Where milk doth so abundant flow,
> Dairyland of Ontario.

Who can say it is not so?

III.—THE WIDER OUTLOOK

And they'll plant churches in the North West,
Where they can serve the Lord the best.

NEVER LIVED POET WHO TOOK A MORE PRACTICAL VIEW
of human affairs than McIntyre, nor who gathered
upon himself less of the cant of art. That is not to
say he was prosaic, unless one is willing to admit—as
I am not — that Tennyson was prosaic when the
romance of industrialism in nineteenth century
England led him to prefer "fifty years of Europe" to
"a cycle of Cathay." As I have tried to make clear in
the cheese section of this study, McIntyre was moved
by cheese as the thing that had brought a large
number of people from misery to joy. It is true he
turned didactic, which is usually considered a peril to
a literary creator's art; but then he made no pretensions
to art. Unlike Gay and Gillis, he disclaimed any great
amount of artistic merit in his writing, saying: "We
are not vain enough to suppose that because we have
produced some lines that said rhymes are poetry. If
we furnish an occasional poetic gleam like a dewdrop
sparkling in the sun, it is all we dare hope for." I
am inclined to think he over-stated his humility; and
certainly cannot agree with his own low estimate of

his performance. His frequent device of double rhyme is clear proof of conscious artifice:

> They must be clad in fur well,
> For it blows cold at Burwell;

And when he ventured into the triple rhymed structures the happier specimens of his ingenuity are beyond praise:

> Other lakes seem inferior
> In size to great Superior.

In so complicated a construction, he is not always up to the mark of the lines just quoted. For instance, I do not care nearly as much for:

> 'Mong choicest fruits you ramble on
> From Niagara to Hamilton,

and, while all will agree that Killicrankie is a much harder word to rhyme than Timbuctoo, which Sir William Gilbert could only match with "hymn-book too", McIntyre's attempt was more courageous than wise:

> And historians will rank the
> Chief highland victory of Killicrankie.

We read McIntyre, however, more for his thought than for his metrics — interesting as they often are. What he grasped was the vital significance of the expansion in his time of farming and manufacturing, and of the improvements in their methods. He did not disdain to write of these things, for they were moulding the lives of the people. He looked on Canada chiefly as the salvation of the tenant farmer, and farm labourer, in Great Britain, as cheese had been the salvation of Ingersoll and vicinity. He was calling people to a better life, and that is the precise function of didactic poetry. His *Donald Ross,* a short narrative, was immigration propaganda forty years before the government established a branch to do that work. The poem concludes:

> He sought a distant strand,
> In Canada bought land,
> To him a glorious charm
> To view his own broad farm,
> His horses and his cows,
> Cultivators and plows,
> **And now** his daughter Flora
> She is the flower of Zorra.

Practical, too, was his patriotism. Like Gay, he addressed an ode to *Governor Lorne and the Princess Louise,* on their arrival in Canada; but he was primarily intent on making this country a good one to live in, and content to let the Royal Family get on without his advice. He was proud of his Scottish birth, yet who can read his poems without seeing that the best part of his heart had been given to his adopted land? The race's future here meant more to him than its past in the British Isles. His song is almost all of Canada, and how it may best be developed into the New Homeland. A pleasant exception, however, is found in the ode written on the occasion of the future King Edward VII embarking for Canada in May, 1860. The similar popularity of his grandson, the later Edward, Prince of Wales, served to keep the sentiment of the old poem fresh, though the reader will notice the quaintly innocent diversions our grandparents were preparing for the entertainment of the royal guest.

WELCOME TO THE PRINCE OF WALES

In his long voyage o'er the sea,
To where doth grow the maple tree,
May he be blest with pleasant gales,
The coming man, the Prince of Wales.

The maple grows but in good soil,
Where nature doth reward for toil;
The farmer splitting his fence rails,
He welcome bids the Prince of Wales.

In the woods the axe is ringing
And the yeomen merry singing,
The sound resounds o'er hills and dales,
Our future king the Prince of Wales.

Round the brow of our future chief
We'll weave a wreath of maple leaf,
For o'er broad Canada prevails
Kind feelings to the Prince of Wales.

When in this land the Prince arrives,
May he have many pleasant drives,
And on our lakes have merry sails,
Great king of princes, Prince of Wales.

McIntyre was a philosopher, as the best poets are, and a realist, as the best philosophers are. He was not

one to go into a pink decline over the abandonment
of obsolete, picturesque methods.   He saw the value
of efficiency, and, for the poetry, realized that a little
extra change in the pocket can jingle a very pretty
tune.   When he wrote of agricultural implements, he
was no sentimentalist:

> Poor labourers they did sad bewail,
> When the machine displaced the flail,
> There's little work now with the hoes,
> Since cultivators weed the rows.
>
> Labour it became more fickle,
> When the scythe took place of sickle,
> Labour still it did sink lower,
> By introduction of mower.
>
> And the work was done much cheaper
> When they added on the reaper,
> Another machine to it they join,
> Mower, reaper, binder, all combine.
>
> Machines now load and stow away,
> Both the barley and the hay,
> And the farmers do get richer
> With the loader and the pitcher.

Thus we see that McIntyre's horizon was wider
than the circumference of the Mammoth Cheese.   He
liked to see anything growing or being made.   For
example:

> The apple, which is queen of fruits,
> Was a good crop and so is roots.

In particular, he had great faith in the development of the Canadian West; and I like to remember

that he lived long enough to see Alberta and Saskatchewan erected into provinces. It must have pleased the old man greatly. Mindful of his own hard experiences in youth, helping to clear the hardwood forests, he expresses perfectly the feelings of the Ontario farmers of that day toward the newly discovered prairie lands. The place seemed to them a farmers' paradise where the plough could be inserted in wild land, and a long, loamy furrow turned without preliminary labour, and a crop could be harvested the first year:

> And while we plow we don't get thumps
> By running it against the stumps.

He had a far-seeing eye, and went so far in his speculations as to the future of the West that once he said: "Winnipeg perchance may be the capital of the Dominion." Optimistic as many Westerners are, and long ago as that was said, it still remains the boldest prediction on the destinies of the newer half of Canada. In the 'eighties, it was a strong thing to say. When he came to prophesy the colonization of the arctic and sub-arctic regions, he was clearly thinking beyond the men around him; and until the last few years there has been no apparent justification for a national outlook as comprehensively sanguine as his. We are not yet as awake to the possibilities of our North as Eastern Canada was to the possibilities of the West forty years ago. For the sake of brevity, I have taken the liberty of making one poem out of scattered stanzas, to show how wide was McIntyre's national thinking. The title also is composite:

CANADA AND ITS FUTURE

Canadian provinces they lay
Divided by river and by bay,
Many a separate division,
Among them there was no cohesion.

But statesmen saw that a great nation
Could be formed by federation,
And soon they led public opinion
To favour forming this Dominion.

Though the North-West is filling slow
Yet soon there will be a mighty flow,
Millions to North-West will hurry
In last decade of century.

For therein is an opening grand
In great fertile prairie land,
For there the choicest wheat it grows
Near where the Saskatchewan flows.

But we sing more glorious theme,
It is our verdant pasture land,
Where cows produce a flood of cream,
Doth make cheese of the finest brand.

From balmy breezes of Lake Erie
To the far north frozen ocean,
Where it now seems lone and dreary,
And will yet be life and motion.

While British blood doth course each vein,
Proudly this heritage maintain,
With fertile acres by the billions,
Future homes of two hundred millions.

Wherever cows come on the scene, be it noted, the poet grows particularly tender. Perhaps what he meant to convey in that last passage was the need the West would soon feel for mixed farming, and a fear which modern scientific agriculturists confirm. There is also to be taken into account the difference between thought and emotion. He understood the greatness awaiting other districs, but his own he loved.

> Some see no beauties near to home,
> But do admire the distant far.
> Each one doth know it is not wise,
> Though our songs may not be vocal,
> Chants of our home for to despise,
> But to prize them 'cause they are local.

This is adequate apology and introduction to the dual section of McIntyre's work entitled *South Ontario Sketches* and *Sketches on the Banks of the Canadian Thames*. The former is represented by part of the poem on St. Thomas, the latter by short extracts from poems on Woodstock, Beachville and Stratford:

> No more need to stay at home as
> There's lots of railroads to St. Thomas,
> You pluckily did boldly venture,
> Now you are great railroad center.
>
> Your city now it hath high hopes
> From its great railway workshops,
> And higher yet it still will rise,
> The seat of so much enterprise.

85

When young man wants a wedded mate
He seeks Alma girl graduate,
And he loves her Alma mater
For the sake of her charming daughter.

* * * *

And through the air there sweetly floats
Harmonious Woodstock organ notes,[1]
And men employment secure
In factory for furniture;
Old Oxford is a seat of knowledge,
Woodstock has a fine new college,
And farm implement work shops,
So farmers easy reap their crops;
The old court house is a disgrace,
Grand structure soon will take its place.

* * * *

Though river here it is not deep,
Yet banks slope graceful up the steep,
And from the summit of the hills
You look down on the famed lime kilns,
And 'tis full worthy poet's rhyme
The whiteness of your pure white lime,
Your glory never shall be gone
While you have quarries of this stone,
In influence you yet will wax
With mills for flour and also flax.

* * * *

For here in Stratford every ward
Is named from dramas of great bard,
Here you may roam o'er Romeo,
Or glance on Juliet bestow.

---

[1]The "Woodstock" reed organ, made at the city of the same name, was one of the most popular musical instruments in use in Ontario at that time, dividing the field with the "Bell" organ, made at Guelph. Gay makes no mention of the "Bell," perhaps because he found his flute sufficient. In the place of honour in the parlor, the organ filled the same function in the Canadian home of the period that the radio and television do now.

The chief poets of England, Scotland and the United States were well known to McIntyre. A substantial section of his book is made up of poems to each of them. As these are mostly polite salutations between bard and bard, they need not be gone into here, beyond selecting two of the shortest to illustrate McIntyre's condensation of utterance. It has been obvious throughout that he does not pad his poems, except for once in a long time when he is at his wits' end for a rhyme: usually he will got to any lengths of inversion, and extend poetic license even to grammar, to avoid the delivery of his message in anything but its most compact form. His refusal of ornamentation is sublime. The career of Shelley came near being reduced to an epigram; and this is the more wonderful because the first line of the quatrain is one of the rare cases of an empty line to fill out the measure:

SHELLEY

We have scarcely time to tell thee
Of the strange and gifted Shelley,
Kind hearted man but ill-fated,
So youthful, drowned and cremated.

WALT WHITMAN

For erratic style he leads van,
Wildly wayward Walt Whitman,
He done grand work in civil war,

For he did dress many a scar,
And kindly wet the hot parched mouth
Of Northern soldiers wounded South.

Shakespeare was his favourite poet; and he had a keen appreciation of the better-known plays. The Baconian theory did not exactly annoy him; but he disbelieved it, and could not see how the genius of the plays would be affected by changing the name of their author. The nature of his reply is indicated in the first stanza of the poem dealing with the point:

Some critics think they do make clear
The fact that Bacon wrote Shakespeare,
But a gent lives in New York
Asks what effect will it have on pork.

The social life of the people, as distinguished from the industrial, does not receive any great amount of the poet's attention. A genial soul, he took manners for granted, and only at rare intervals, and usually incidentally, is there any mention of them. One of the few examples recalls the buggy-riding that then formed one of the chief mechanical aids to courtship:

FEMALE REVENGE

I heard Bill say to-day, Mary,
That you are a charming fairy,
And that to town he'd give you drive,
But just as sure as you're alive,
He does intend to have the bliss,
Of stealing from your lips a kiss.

I'll let him drive me now, Jane,
His efforts. they will all be vain,
I hate him, and I him defy,
And anger flashed from her eye,
The monster's wiles I will defeat,
Peck of strong onions I will eat.

Finally there are many ballads, and without some
acquaintance with these the student's knowledge of
McIntyre is insufficient. To illustrate this phase of
his art I have selected three, of which the first is quoted
in part only, and the last two in full. These narratives
—pathetic, tender and dramatic—need no comment.

THE GATES AJAR

A good kind man who knew no malice,
Happy with wife and daughter Alice,
More precious far to him than gold,
His little darling six years old.

True nobleman with many friends,
His career too soon it ends,
The casket friends enshrined with flowers,
While soul had fled to heavenly bowers.

The wreaths were lovely, but the star,
Admired by all was gates ajar,
The widow led her little girl
To where death his dart did hurl.

And stricken her poor father down,
But the child exclaimed he's won the crown,
And he will watch for me afar,
And keep for me the gates ajar.

89

Pa will admit his little Alice
Safe into the heavenly palace,
And glories to me will unfold
As we tread the streets of gold.

EVERY ROSE HATH ITS THORN

There was a maiden all forlorn,
She loved a youth, his name was Thorn,
But he was shy for to disclose
How he loved dear the sweet May Rose.

Lustre sweet it would give to Thorn,
If this fair flower would it adorn,
Said he all other names above
Your charming name alone I love.

Said she of beauty 'tis soon shorn,
Unless that it be joined to Thorn,
It very soon doth droop and die,
And she heaved a gentle sigh.

Said he we'll wed tomorrow morn,
No more from me shall you be torn,
For you will banish all my woes,
And near my heart I'll wear the rose.

Now little rose buds they are born,
All clinging to the parent Thorn,
In grace and beauty each one grows,
Full worthy of the sweet May Rose.

Some flowers they only shed their bloom
In the sweet month of leafy June,
But May doth bloom each month in year
A fragrant Rose forever dear.

LOST SON FOUND

An English ship when homeward bound,
Near to its port was shipwrecked found,
For it had struck a sunken rock,
And was slowly sinking from the shock.

In port they quick did man life boat,
Which o'er tempestuous sea did float,
They rescued all the crew, save one,
And were content with what they done.

But they had not their captain, Harry,
Who on the shore was forced to tarry,
And knew not of the disaster,
So crew had worked without a master.

But when he heard of the shipwreck,
And that a man was left on deck,
He quickly hurried the boat's crew
For to again attempt his rescue.

But earnestly his old mother,
Reminded him of his lost brother,
Perhaps drowned in a foreign sea,
She cried, son, stay and comfort me.

But wreck they reach and rescue man,
And thrill of joy o'er city ran,
When it was found 'twas Harry's brother,
Had returned to comfort mother.

Thus providence rewards the brave
Who strive their fellow men to save,
The mother's griefs it did assuage,
And happy now is her old age.

James D. Gillis: a Man of Parts

Here thought moves in labour

JAMES D. GILLIS IS A MAN OF LETTERS, HAVING PUBLISHED books of both prose and verse, also a text book on grammar for use in the schools, and prepared a simplified map of the world. He will soon issue his first work of fiction; and the considerable number of delighted readers he has acquired almost ensures any book written by him a reasonable circulation.

Judged by commercial success, Gillis is the most considerable figure in this series of studies. Since *The Cape Breton Giant* appeared in 1898, there has been a continuous demand for his work, requiring several editions to fill; and as this is being written I learn that still another printing is in immediate prospect, for the book gains in popularity yearly. The New York Public Library is guarding one copy, and recently a friend of mine met a man on a train who had had his bound in flexible leather that he might carry it constantly as a pocket companion, from which to refresh himself in moments otherwise idle, or at times of mental depression. Mr. William T. Allen said lately in an interview that the demand for it was "perfectly surprising." An order from Detroit came in while the interview was taking place, and Mr. Allen mentioned having recently received orders from Alaska and India. The author himself mentions correspondence from Honolulu and other distant points.

This masterpiece I have reserved for a separate chapter, on account of its size and importance, and must here prepare the way for its reception by telling something of the author's life, illustrated by quotations from his volume of poems, which is entitled *The Great Election*. The minor works will be dealt with more briefly in chronological sequence.

In Gillis's native island of Cape Breton, Scottish people are in the overwhelming majority, numbering more than the English, Irish and French combined; and his story really begins about the year 1800, when a colony of two thousand Scots migrated to Cape Breton. Some of these played prominent parts in the political struggle of 1832, which forms the base of the epic, *The Great Election*. That Gillis's own ancestor was one of the two thousand we may infer from the vehemence of his denial that the migrants had been driven out of Scotland as a result of the Jacobite rising of 1745, though many of them were Roman Catholics. Two men by the name of Gillis are mentioned as active in that election of 1832—John, who "voted at the three poles," and

> The fertile Angus Gillis,

who must have been responsible for the almost unbelievable number of people with that surname now inhabiting that part of the world. Which man was James D.'s direct ancestor is not known; but the name is so common that the author is compelled to add to his name the designation, Teacher, to distinguish himself from others of exactly the same name.

"I was born," he says in the Preface to *The Cape Breton Giant,* "on July 11th, 1870, at Strathlorne, not far from the residence of John MacIsaac, Donald's son." And lately he has stated: "I was born at Broad Cove Intervale, July 11th, 1871." The discrepancy is in the date only, for the two villages are less than four miles apart, and in such cases farmers situated midway often refer to themselves alternately as of the one place or the other. As to the date, I am inclined to believe the earlier statement, and that the later was a slip of the pen, since 1870 agrees better with other dates and periods of years he speaks of.

At the time of my birth I had my first teeth and some jokingly predicted that I was a poet to be. Malcolm McLellan, a graduate of the Free Mason College of Kirkcudbright, Scotland, said I was the image of Sir Walter Scott.

His parents had originally homesteaded at Grand Mira. His father was a house painter and blacksmith, also a "noted violinist and piper and a wit." The author's mother, through whom he doubtless derived his taste for writing, was born Christina Macaulay. She was descended from the Macaulays of North Uist, and was a distant relative of Lord Macaulay.

James was the youngest of a family of four—Johanna, Angus Martin, Elizabeth Jane and James Donald. His brother and both sisters seem to have predeceased him, as he has now no living relatives closer than cousins. His birthplace was by the sea, on the northern part of Cape Breton Island, and on the western coast. His father died when James was seven months old, and he was taken to the home of an uncle at Upper Margaree, where he grew up. This village is six or seven miles inland from his birthplace, and on the Margaree River, near Lake Ainslie, in which the river has its source. It was doubtless from youthful observations on the banks of this stream that he came later to frame the suggestive line:

> The salmon gloats on his vacation.

Apart from details of his education, nothing is known of his boyhood, unless the normally healthy appetite of that period is reflected in the passage in one of his poems, which runs:

> . . . to draw
> Us vim and strength
> From those fat beefsteaks
> And those subtle hot buns
> That melting in the mouth
> Delight the weary mind.

He was an infant prodigy. At the age of five he was in Grade IV, and at six in Grade VI. His is not the first case in which a genius has appeared fully equipped for his life work, and has shown distaste for the ordinary school-room grind that other children endure uncomplainingly, and apparently with benefit. These experiences, however, are better told in the author's own words:

> In those days I learned or in reality showed insidious comprehension and invention of probable causes of things &c to which no schools or books since have added an iota.
>
> Before the age of twelve I was a better grammarian and composer than I am today. Yet no school teacher of those days would likely approve of my parsing or idioms of expression. I followed function and necessity and never recognized authority. When older I noticed that many of the shackles of language were relics of the persecution of Greece and Rome.
>
> At the age of eighteen I became proficient enough to teach school. . . .

This takes us down to the year 1888; and the first school over which the author presided was at Broad Cove Banks, within a very short distance of his birthplace. For the next sixteen years he taught in a succession of rural schools in the vicinity, and devoted himself to the preparation of *The Cape Breton Giant,* which was published in 1898, when the author was teaching in the Kiltarlity School.

While most of his life has been spent in the school room, he speaks of interpersing other occupations with his teaching, but assigns no dates. He worked for short periods on a farm and in a saw mill, and was also for a time established in an insane asylum as an attendant. If he happened to be on night duty in that institution at the time of composing his "life" of MacAskill, the long hours of quiet and comparative inactivity would provide suitable occasions for the composing of the work, which bears signs of having been written in protracted sittings. It may equally have been the work of a vacation; but the uniformity of style, and the plan of continuity, point to its having been no piece-meal job.

The next six years were spent in teaching and in compiling *The Canadian Grammar*, which was published at North Sydney, N.S., in 1904. So far as is known, this has never been adopted by the department of education in any province. For the general reader, it lacks the originality and force of other compositions, and draws rather too freely from the authorized textbook then in use, though it is not without ample evidence of its author's personality. As an able critic has said: "While not so coruscating with gems as the *Giant*, it contains much of interest to the connoisseur." Many buy it, not so much for thorough reading as to possess a complete set of the author's works. Yet there is many a memorable sentence in the *Grammar*, and it repays perusal.

In the following year, 1905, while still continuing to teach, Gillis set himself to solve the intricate problem of simplifying the study of geography. He wished to remove the mathematical complications arising from the curved surface of the earth; and eventually he managed to work it out by imposing the continents upon a flat ground. To do this, he had to invent two extra poles, and is rather proud of the fact that his East and West Poles are both on land—the former, called Gillis's Pole, is situate in Borneo, and the latter in South America. Thus there is east and west latitude as well as north and south, and all is regular and straight sailing. "All the latitude lines E. & W.," he explains, "may be mathematically regarded as straight lines and in another sense are not what they are but what they represent. They represent distances not curves." This labour took him a year. By 1906 the details of this revolutionary map had all been worked out, and the author employed A. E. DesBrisay of Halifax to make the original drawing, and several blue prints of it.

It has been erroneously supposed that Gillis adheres to the "flat earth" theory, which has numerous supporters in England; but his theory is that a triangle on a curved surface has the same area as a plane surface triangle, and he might therefore do away with the (to children) confusing converging longitudinal lines of the maps now used. That he is not a "flat earther" is indicated by a passage in *The Cape Breton Giant*:

As for Cabot and others, previous to Columbus' discovery, they had never dreamt of the roundness or roundity of the earth. but our great benefactor, Columbus, studied physiography for years. At length he concluded that the earth was round. . . .

About this time the author decided to secure further qualifications in his profession, and attended the Normal College at Truro for the year 1907-08, at the end of which he graduated. He says: "That was a happy year," and that he was "treated well there" by most of the instructors, but in particular by Mr. Benoit, Dr. Soloan and Dr. Hall.

> Drs. Soloan and Hall encouraged me in literature and inventions. Both seemed amazed at my genius. I thought Dr. Soloan a wonderful man. I would be inclined to class him with Comenius, Scipio, Luther and Napoleon.

The "Mr. Benoit" was J. Alphonse Benoit, a most correct young French Acadian, who then taught trigonometry. Gillis, who has always been independent and tenacious in his views, was brought up on that old classic, *Chambers's Practical Mathematics*, which he knew well. A problem set the class elicited from him a lengthy and complicated method of working, which Mr. Benoit criticized as too lengthy. Gillis rose with indignation against a Nova Scotian, and not even an English-blooded one, who dared to put himself as superior to the great Chambers. Smilingly, Mr. Benoit retorted by calling on the class to pass judgment on his method in contrast to Gillis's. With a voice like one roaring down a rain-barrel, the Cape Bretonian objected: " 'Tis the first time I ever heard a mathematical problem being decided by a popular vote."

Part of the next year, which was 1909, Gillis spent at Dalhousie University. It is gratifying to know that the young author came under the stimulating influence of Professor Archibald MacMechan, who has shown a particular interest in native literature, and who, as head of the English department, probably gave the young author further encouragement. In a recent interview, Gillis said:

I learned some there but except Dr. Eben McKay's and Dr. MacMechan's, I could not appreciate the method of teaching.

Despite this graceful tribute, Gillis soon left the University, and there is probably some truth in the report that he once said disdainfully that he learned more standing on a street corner in Boston in an hour than he did at Dalhousie the whole three months he was there. Also, this may have been the literal truth, for one does not derive much benefit from college lectures covering only a few weeks. There is nothing to mark the date of the trip to Boston, except that a reference in the Preface to *The Cape Breton Giant* implies that he had travelled in his youth before its publication:

I was twice to the United States: I do not say so for the sake of boast.

A story is also attributed to him that he once received a low mark in geometry, and asking the professor the reason for it, was told that it was because his paper was full of errors, whereupon Gillis is supposed to have replied that he had noticed Euclid was full of mistakes, but failed to see why he should be punished for it. Disagreement from Euclid is an advanced style in mathematics, with which my aging brain cannot cope. An eminent engineer of my acquaintance has tried in vain to make me understand the principles of non-Euclidian geometry; but I think I grasp the nature of the difficulty between Gillis and Euclid. Any reader of Gillis's work knows that he does not accept the axiom that a straight line is the shortest distance between two points. He has a horror of direct statement, and comes to his revelations by mysterious, circuitous paths. Take the lines.

> I pass by the home of my love in the valley
> The thought is a joy, that your voice will increase.

Ordinarily, those words would mean that, while passing the house, the poet was glad that the lady's voice was increasing—presumably in volume, as from vocal training, but possibly in beauty. What it actually means is that the poet's joy in passing the house will be increased when he returns to the house and hears the voice of his loved one. These tricks of inversion are something for which the reader of Gillis's more difficult passages must always be on the alert. He asserts:

> Early in life I came to conclusions some of which I notice in present books on geometry.

It is, of course, a wonderful feat for this self-taught Cape Bretonian to have anticipated Einstein by some five years in his discovery of relativity. That he did so, accounts for his quarrel with the now obsolete Euclid; and that he did so, and by 1916 understood the compound space-time factor, is proved conclusively by this passage, published at that time:

> I thought I was gone in the days of arrival
> To find that again
> We had met with ourselves.

What it means is beyond my intellect, since I have already confessed to a most vague notion about such things as curved space; but (I confess it with some chagrin) I recognize the time element to be in harmony with the doctrines of relativity because of a silly limerick some wag made up soon after Einstein had published his book:

> There was a young lady named Bright,
> Whose speed was much faster than light.
> She went off one day,
> In a relative way,
> And returned on the previous night.

Fame had been assured by his first book. But he had not then, nor has he yet, reaped sufficient monetary return from his books to enable him to face the future carelessly. By the time his vocational training was complete he was thirty-nine years of age. Two books were out, and the map was done. But ten years were to elapse after the completion of the map and before he should startle the world with another book. With the patience of his race, he returned to his schools, and laboured for his country in the all-important post of rural school-master for five precious years. No inspiration came to him. The initial excitement over the success of his great book had worn off. It was the Black Night of the Soul. Then, perhaps it was, that the thought first came to him which was later to be enshrined in one of his own poems:

> When Victory crowns the world applauds
> When failure comes there's naught but God.

It was not failure. It was only a rest period: Fate was storing up further experience to tutor his wisdom. In 1914 the Great War broke out. Gillis had enlisted in the 94th Militia Regiment in 1894, and had held a Cadet Instruction Certificate since 1909; and had taught military drill in his schools. Like a true Scot, he rushed to the colours:

> I dote on the wars as my father before me
> I dream of promotions that seldom befall.

That was not in all respects a happy experiment. The author was forty-four years old; and he had always loved personal freedom too well to be able to submit to army discipline without an inner struggle. For two years he drilled; twice he was on the point of leaving with his unit, only to be disappointed on each occasion; and finally, in 1916, he returned to civilian life.

It was far from a case of all being lost save honour. During his leisure hours in camp he had completed another book—poems this time—and on his discharge rushed off to North Sydney to arrange for publication. This *opus* was *The Great Election,* from which I have drawn the numerous poetical quotations scattered through this chapter. Then, too, army life does something to a man: he cannot as a rule settle back into his niche quite contentedly—sometimes, he cannot return at all. So it was with Gillis. The compulsion to change of scene was in his blood, not to be denied. Canada's great West called him; and for the following six years he dwelt on the prairies, far from the beautiful country he had made his own between Upper Margaree and MacAskill's former home at St. Ann, thirty miles east, on the Atlantic side of the Island.

For a part of that time he was a watchman at the Robert Simpson Company's store in Regina; but the greater part of it was spent in much the same sort of teaching he had done at home. His comment on the educational system of the Western Provinces is pithy:

I have taught school for 37 years and six of these in Sask. & Alta. I liked teaching in the West taking hold of several schools that were in poor shape and left them in good style. I taught among British, Canadians, Austrians, Germans and Ukranians.

I preferred to live among the latter. The Ukranians were like brothers to me. The great barrier in the West is the attitude of Inspectors. In Sask. & Alta. if there were no Inspectors, those provinces would be equal to Montana and Illinois. The system of Ontario has threshed out all ambition and originality. Of what good is a visit from an Inspector that doesn't take place unless there's a complaint made, and otherwise comes but once a year and likely at an undesirable time?

Since his return to Cape Breton in 1922, he has put in five more quiet years teaching, broken only by a term at the Summer School in 1926 for further training. During the school year 1926-27 he taught at South Highlands, Inverness County. But these years have also borne fruit, since I am privileged to announce that another book from his pen may be expected shortly.

I intend to issue a biography—fiction—before long. Besides being of general interest, I trust it will be a guide to young people and will I hope check the Anti-christs, leadership, vogues, life jobs, cowardly (professional) reports and perfidy.

All who have read his former work will be looking forward with keenest anticipation to the publication of the new book, that sounds so promising. It is sure to be inspiring, and he always prefers an atmosphere in which, to use his own phrase, "realities are rife."

Asked what pastimes he indulged in, the author replied: "Playing the violin and bagpipe, mathematics and reading, visiting and conversation, climbing mountains, &c. I can fish, swim and walk on stilts." He does not use tobacco nor any kind of intoxicating liquors. Shy and sensitive, he has tramped alone the roads between Broad Cove on the West Coast and North Shore, a village north of St. Ann, on the East Coast of the Island; and he knows and loves every foot of that enchanting district. As he wanders about, he calls on his many friends in the farm houses and villages, who are always glad to entertain him at a meal, or put him up for the night, both because he is well liked for himself, and because his music is always welcome.

Canny in the extreme, he never takes any one into his confidence as to his intended destinations. As the old hymn runs, he "moves in a mysterious way his wonders to perform." A visitor who was recently looking him up had a long chase. Knowing the author was in the immediate neighbourhood—between Why-cocomagh and North Sydney—and often hearing that he had just passed this or that point, the stranger yet spent several hours driving in his car before he found the man he was seeking. The visitor's report of the experience is worth recording:

Finally we heard the faint strains of *Scots wha hae wi' Wallace Bled* wafted over the evening air, and knew that we had run our quarry to earth. Gillis is a man with a fine sensitive mind, and seems to be a likeable chap. He is a piper and violinist, and after our chat was very pleased to play for a while. As he sat there with his eyes closed, his fine wide forehead and sensitive face in complete repose, and quite oblivious to his surroundings, playing selection after selection from his evident abundant store of sweet and expressive old Scotch airs, while the great summer sun slowly sank behind Loch Ban, it gave the whole meeting a deep sensitive personal touch of kindliness not easily forgotten. I am glad to have met him, and if you ever come this way I think you would enjoy a visit to that part of the country.

This sketch is obviously—nay, glaringly—lacking in its omission of any mention of the author's emotional life—particularly in his relations with the ladies. He never married, nor has he ever explained the reason. That his abstinence from matrimony has been due to no lack of amativeness we infer from his racial inheritance and artistic temperament. One need not cite the example of Burns to realize that it is impossible for a Scottish poet to have gone through life without being in love; and his poetry confirms this hypothesis. For a peculiar thing has happened here. Whereas in his prose, which is the language of restraint, he betrays his passionate love of the scenery of his district in many lyrical passages verging on ecstasy; his poetry, which is the language of abandon, is almost devoid of any allusion to the scenic splendours with which the poet is surrounded, and their natural place in the scheme is taken by many verses to girls in general and in particular, and to the glorification of the love of man for maid.

To illustrate this from his writings, compare any of

the descriptions of landscape in *The Cape Breton Giant*
with the barrenness of scenic detail in the following:

> Whycocomagh dost thou remember
> When the swelling crowds
> Moved to and from thee
> Pointing north in famous '32?

The scenery at Whycocomagh, a village fifteen miles
due south of Upper Margaree, is just as captivating as
that at any other point in the district. Descriptions
of scenery have taken so large a place in Canadian
poetry that Gillis's failure to show interest is the more
noticeable. Their place is taken by visions like this:

> And lovely girls
> In pink ado
> With costumes swell
> Enrich the view.

Repressed in the prose, the author's natural longings
are released under the stimulus of the rhythms of
his verse. His desire for Ellen is expressed with happy
freedom:

> I'm dutiful to pa and ma
> My daily toil it passes, O,
> Its studies hard would miss reward
> Were I denied the lasses, O.
>
> Her voice would metaphor excel,
> Her face is ruby flashes, O,
> Let others praise the belles of old,
> Give me my age's lasses, O.

108

The number of the names used in poems of this class suggests that Gillis may not have married because unable to choose among the hosts of his charmers. Or, this factor may have been combined with one aspect of the pronounced caution characteristic of his attitude to other things, and recalling the sad case of Immanuel Kant. It was the great Scottish-German philosopher's rule to consider every matter fully before committing himself by word or act. Twice he contemplated marriage; but he did it so long and carefully that in the one case the lady had become engaged to another man while the philosopher was making up his mind to ask her, and in the other case the lady had moved away from Konigsberg, and so out of Kant's life forever, by the time he had decided to propose. Gillis had the advantage of Kant in being able to console himself in writing poems to those he loved and lost:

RUTH ANNIE

Attired in Eaton's latest
She's just a sight to view;
Her sprightly step is music,
And art attained by few
Her talk is light and free,
And healthful as the breeze
That roams the broad Atlantic,—
    She's life or death to me.

For years you've been my study,—
I labour but to earn
A moment with Ruth Annie
Among yon shaded ferns.

109

Then fairest maid my glee
Is perfect joy with thee,—
O there I see Ruth Annie,—
She's life or death to me.

Ruth Annie differs from Ellen in being an actual
person. Gillis has considerately supplied prose notes
to these poems, from which we learn the identities of
Ruth Annie, Miss McKay, Bonny Birdie and Molly;
and he adds that "the other (love) poems are alle-
gorical." The footnote on Miss McPhail reads:

The subject of the foregoing was Ruth Annie McPhail, of
Scotsville. She is one of an excellent family. A sister, Mary Ann,
died in the United States some years ago. She too was an
estimable lady.

Continuing to quote in part only from the various
love poems and their attendant notes, we are rewarded
with glimpses of Miss McKay and Bonny Birdie:

MISS McKAY

I regret to see you go, Miss McKay;
Other hearts are sad I know, Miss McKay;
But we must be all resigned,
Lest our patience fall behind;
Yet, we'll miss your face so kind, Miss McKay.

Miss McKay, can't you stay, Miss McKay,
O my heart is sad today, Miss McKay;
For your voice it was so kind
That with grief I'm almost blind
To reflect I'm left behind, Miss McKay.

But our loss is Boston's gain, Miss McKay;
You will lead in beauty's train, Miss McKay;
Uncle Sam will sing your praise—
Sing your merits and your ways,
Till you find that virtue pays, Miss McKay.

The subject of the foregoing was Christy Ann McKay, of Scotsville, later Mrs. Duncan MacMillan. She was beautiful and talented. Two brothers served in the Cuban campaign. A brother, John, was a good scholar and an excellent reader.

BONNY BIRDIE

A maid who dwells on yonder hill
Is certain cure for all my ills
And sure, I never loved until
 I met my charming Birdie.

Her toilet's in the height of taste
Despite domestic cares and haste;
And O to span the artless waist—
 The tempting waist of Birdie.

The subject of the foregoing was Jessie Ann Dunbar (better known as Birdie Dunbar). Both she and Mr. Gillis were youthful at that time. The scene is Lake Ainslie.

The devotion of which the poet is capable is seen to even better advantage in the lines to Molly—Molly Gunn as she then was, now Mrs. R. McLeod of Inverness. Here, in the complete liberty of the free verse form, the poet was able to ascend in his most daring and successful flight. That swift up-rush is a breathless performance: it stops for nothing, revealing a poet inspired by the quintessence of passion and sure of his wings. His technique, forgotten, allows the poet a moment of divinely creative power:

FIRST POET

For Beauty likes to linger in the past
And also in distant birds of passage
And sometimes it graces new acquaintances
Then dissolves
But now and then we find it
Where expected as in the face
And form of Molly.
Who shall presume to portray
The healthy face?
The rainbow's self
Alone can illustrate the
Variegated congress of Nature's touches
That adorn the form
And face of lovely Molly
As o'er the piano's snow-white keys
Her whiter hands doth glide.
Her fingers like the Aurora
Playing in a ruby sky.
The western winds caress her
The eastern gales subside
When intoxicated with her breath.

As an artist in the medium of prose, Gillis receives attention in the following chapter. It is convenient, however, to touch immediately on a few general considerations of his art in verse. The first point is his astonishing versatility. While *The Great Election* is a narrative of a fight at the polls, all sorts of other topics are woven into the story, as must have been already evident to the reader from the quotations employed in this chapter. The poet does not exaggerate when he outlines his panoramic and kaleidoscopic picture:

> . . . imagination recalls
> Learning, trade, adventures,
> Hospitality, inspectorates,
> African battlefields
> And the like
> Withal beautiful music

Again I have to remark on the amazing attraction of elegaic themes for Canadian poets, and their high attainments in this sort of poetry. Gillis has published contributions, and, like *Molly*, it is done in free verse, only one threnody; but that is among his most notable. Too long for full quotation, it begins:

A DEATH

> He is gone.
> We shall weep. We ease our minds
> By opening the throttle
> That suppresses our feelings
> There he lies.

There is another line I would quote, too, which strikes me as remarkable for its characteristic of deferred, or hesitating, alliteration, here used for the first time in literature. How much more delicate an effect it gives than the usual practice of running the alliterative words all together noisily!

Loftiest beauty lit her lowly gait.

113

Questioned about his methods of composition, the poet graciously replied:

I write best in quiet places, groves preferred in summer. The faster I write the better. But I need some cause. I must be satisfied as to the wisdom of the logic before I can write with brilliancy. I find no difficulty in giving sentences punch if the succession of points is consistent and the thought deep and far reaching.

He must have been writing at top speed when composing the following lines. The student will observe that the impelling topic is again the mating-call theme:

The mutual love of either sex
Is seldom reckoned ere they come
It comes in power virtue decked
And threatens oft the wisest plans
The world is often unprepared
To meet this passion's quick demands.

Gillis's work as a whole illustrates repeatedly his candor and hatred of compromise. One of his sagest thoughts in this vein is:

But does the Child of Moderation
E'er rise above mediocrity?

All Gillis's thought is virile. Independence of viewpoint distinguishes most of his utterances; and to this is united a most liberal outlook. In politics he favours the Liberal Party, and is an anti-Confederation man, on the grounds that Confederation has proved detrimental to the Maritime Provinces. His heroes are all strong men—Cromwell, James I and VI, Cæsar, Wellington, and Napoleon I, William Wallace, James Wolfe, General Amherst, Peperel, Louis Riel and General Foch. Under the heading "modern reformers," he signifies his admiration for Lenin and Trotski. It matters not to him that the last two are popularly considered monsters in this country: Bolsheviks or not, they were successful, and anyway Gillis is no timorous upholder of the *status quo*:

> Let useless humility
> And cursed subordination
> Be no more.

Napoleon, whose career Gillis has studied deeply, he endorses up to the point where he ceased to be a servant of the people, and became their master:

> He a lover of peace
> A patron of discoveries, schools,
> Churches and arts
> From his aptitude for wars
> Found himself yearly
> In the very crater
> Of his millenium's convulsion.

> * * * *

> Yet Napoleon surely went too far.
> Shall we today have one or more
> Dictate to us? No.
> We're neither slaves nor mendicants.

Bravely spoken! And if our institutions, even the oldest of them, have outlived their usefulness, let us not be sentimental over them because of their age, but manfully devise some other system. It takes more courage to say a good word for the Soviet Republics in our day than it did for the English poets to approve of the French and Italian revolutions between 1775 and 1850.

> That Parliament essential is
> And Socialists must bow to this,
> What nonsense!
> A crowd of men that know their work
> Require no foreman's jarring shout.
>
>   *   *   *   *
>
> Those duties, taxes, all together,
> Are nothing but the worst oppression.

We shall see the same radical tendencies being expressed otherwise in the next chapter. But here let us leave him for the present—playing his Scotch airs at sunset, guarding the right of free speech by free exercise of it in candid criticism, watching over his children, and, as circumstances permit, adding to the series of books in which his fellow-countrymen take a unique pride.

The Cape Breton Giant

I.—GILLIS, THE ARTIST

There is not a settlement in the Dominion of Canada, or in the United States, that is not aware of the fact that there once lived a man by the name of Angus MacAskill, who was a prodigy of size and strength. As an infant, he was, as said elsewhere, but of average size and nobody dreamt of the bustle his future prodigious size and appalling strength were to occasion throughout the whole world, civilized and uncivilized, (from pole to pole).

Now this book gives all the important events of MacAskill's career in language, which, if sometimes florid, is none the less easily understood by all who are fairly versed in the language of England. The author is satisfied that this work is virtually a superb representative of MacAskill's greatness. The author is confident that it will be found more interesting than a fairy tale. Applicable quotations sparkle here and there, and where convenient are credited to their authors. The portraits make the book still more valuable, so that this biography is the very best of its kind that was ever published.

JAMES D. GILLIS, TEACHER, RATES HIS MASTERPIECE, *The Cape Breton Giant,* none too highly. If anything, it is the prior fame of MacAskill that he exaggerates. At the time he wrote, what he says of his hero's reputation was possibly true; but it is a truism that the world has a short memory for its idols; and MacAskill's

117

present fame he owes entirely to the literary skill of his biographer, which is yearly spreading that fame wider and ever wider. It is fortunate that the book's appearance at the end of the last century served to acquaint the rising generation, and the hordes of immigrants settling in Western Canada, with the mighty Cape Bretonian, whose immortality is now assured.

But it is not for the sake of the giant, so much as for the author's sprightly prose, that this "life" has enjoyed a vogue extending over half a century. In this, Gillis bears a striking resemblance to Walter Pater. We read them both, not so much for the information conveyed as for the marvellously fluent English, the delightful backgrounds, and stately, philosophic reflections by the way.

In 1898 the Montreal *Family Herald and Weekly Star* printed an article by C. H. Campbell of Riverside, California, about Angus MacAskill, the greatest giant of Cape Breton, who had died thirty-five years earlier. On reading this, Murdoch MacLean of Upper East Ainslie suggested to James D. Gillis the need for a full-dress biography, which the latter undertook, and executed, gathering his material from local legends and from persons still living who had known the "Big Boy." With MacAskill's life I shall deal later, as the more important thing is that his history inspired Gillis and got him to writing. The imagination of Gillis was

inflamed by the size of his subject. He experienced
hero-worship at its purest and most intense. Cultivating
an heroic style to harmonize with the dimensions of
MacAskill, Gillis let his genius have free play with the
result that he produced the most remarkable prose work
ever composed on Canadian soil.

It is fortunate that the giant's life was not more
eventful, and that Gillis did not have more data at his
disposal; for it is the personality of the author that
counts in bellelettristic writing, rather than the theme,
and the less precise his information about MacAskill,
the more he had to draw from himself. Just as we
read *The French Revolution* for the favour of Carlyle,
regardless of how interesting his facts may be in themselves, so we read *The Cape Breton Giant* for Gillis
rather than MacAskill, and are richly repaid.

A hack might have completed the biography in two
printed pages, or five at most. Gillis, using every known
device of padding (and some hitherto unexploited)
swelled his narrative to a grand total of ninety-five
pages. Scenic descriptions, moral precepts, encyclo-
pædic broadsides of historical and geographical facts,
and shrewd observations on a hundred irrelevant matters, help out the main thread, and, what is more
important, allow the author's mind and soul a fulness
of self-expression that is deeply satisfying to the reader
no less than to the author. So I call Gillis artist first
because his masterpiece contains a higher percentage of

extraneous matter than any other book, and second because of his style—now Jamesian in its prolixity, now Stevensonian in its colloquial and conversational ease and gracefulness, but always essentially, and at its noblest, pure Gillisian and inimitable.

Take MacAskill's visit to Edinburgh, which occupies an entire chapter of four pages. The giant is mentioned only in two sentences, telling that he had held in his hand the sword of Sir William Wallace. This was evidently the only known fact. The rest of the space is used in narrating the career of Wallace, which is all made to lead up to the revelation about MacAskill handling the sword. He also visited Dumfries on the same trip; but as that excursion did not yield even a sword incident, the author contents himself with this neat summary of the life, works and character of Burns:

But a few words about Dumfries City. Here lies buried one of Scotland's intellectual giants, Robert Burns. He was a great poet. Notwithstanding his naturally strong and rebellious passions, he lived a good life, a life of current sobriety, a life of superfluous honesty, and died happily, attended by his wife, bonnie Jean, and by his lovely friend, Jessie Lewyars.

How suggestive that is in its concision! And like unto it is the passage wherein ten miles of scenery is compressed into three sentences, as a futurist painter might with as many lines create the illusion of depth and shade—calling up, by his austere magic, myriad hints of forests and vistas and fleeting midsummer clouds:

> From Baddeck to St. Ann's the miles number ten. The road is good. On the way you pass by an I.O.G.T. Lodge.[1]

Like Washington Irving in *Knickerbocker's New York*, Gillis gets a running start at his subject by reviewing the discovery of America, during which survey he sagely remarks:

> It is of little interest to refer to that discovery of America by the Northmen. It was at best a slipshod affair, and resulted in songs which our ordinary people of this day could not understand.

Rhythm in prose is one of the least understood phases of the art of writing. Gillis's mastery of it is seen to advantage in a fragment touching on his hero's muscular powers:

> Our hero often merited and enjoyed the applause of ladies and gentlemen by passing swiftly over the sidewalk with two barrels of salted pork, one under each arm.

To appreciate fully the word harmony of this sentence it should be read aloud, deliberately, with careful enunciation of each phrase, and giving each word its full tonal value. If this exercise is repeated five or six times, the reader will find that those words will never forsake his memory. When an author can perform the

---

[1] For the benefit of readers in foreign lands, I add an accurate explanation of the nature of the activities of the Independent Order of Good Templars, given on a subsequent page of Gillis's book: "The object of those ladies and gentlemen who meet here is to suppress intemperance." The order has been disbanded.

miracle of arranging words in such a manner that they leave an indelible impress upon a reader's mind, that author has found his place among the immortals. There are lines of Milton, and even some of Shakespeare's, that I have forgotten; but some of Gillis's will remain with me forever. On a street-car, or while smoothing out my mind prior to sleep, there will appear in it suddenly and entire a sentence from Gillis, like a star in an evening sky—complete in itself and magnificent, apparently unrelated to anything else in the universe— and I face old age with equanimity, rejoicing in the compensatory law that life having deprived me of much has yet given me Gillis to marvel at, and comfort me in these over-sophisticated days with a sense of wonder and awe.

There is only one name for the manner in which Gillis writes—that hackneyed tag, "the grand style." He acknowledges his style to be "florid"; but of course it is more than that: under stress of the author's passion it soars like an airplane, indulges in the most difficult and dangerous manœuvres, and always returns from these flights under perfect control. The level stretches are cleverly spaced to afford the necessary relief from the dizzy heights to which he periodically climbs by labyrinthine ways of the air, known to himself alone. For at its best, Gillis's style impresses one not so much by its altitudes as by its convolutions. It is thrilling to witness him extricate himself from some of the more tortuous constructions he enters with perfect assurance.

And like those who have employed the grand style before him, the mighty masters of by-gone ages, Gillis is only able to manipulate language as he does because he maintains a perfect gravity. Never did author turn his back more resolutely upon froth, humour and idle vanities of that sort. He uses as subtitle "A TRUTHFUL MEMOIR"; and one feels even a trifle repelled, at times, before the severity of which his people are capable in their most earnest moments. Yet his grim determination to tell the truth, come what may, and to put all levity aside, is the source of that secret strength that sustains him in his greatest passages.

A great critic has said that absolute originality is essential to any work of art, since, without it, the composition can only be a copy or paraphrase of the real work of art. This requisite of the artist Gillis displays lavishly on every page. Given a sentence, or even a paragraph from his work, it is impossible to guess what he is going to say next. Or if the gist of any passage were given to a group composed of I do not care what famous living authors, not one of them would express the thought in phrases anything like those Gillis himself uses. His skill as a phrase-maker is proved by the way his happier expressions now pass as current coin in the speech of the Maritime Provinces.

How does he carry himself under the burden of his great powers? With humility enough to recognize his own importance, which is surely nobler than affecting ignorance of his genius. What he has written of Mac-Askill on this point, applies equally to Gillis himself:

As already observed, it was the fortune of our hero that he was not swayed overmuch by vanity. Of course he duly appreciated the praise of his admirers but not to excess. On the contrary this power of the mind is essential in the mental organism. But, like the other faculties, it requires Providential grace, for its suitable enlivenment and a grace-pervaded reason or understanding for its guidance and moderation. Given these akin to essential requisites, vanity is a treasure.

II.—THE STORY OF MacASKILL

ANGUS MACASKILL'S PARENTS AND HIS TWELVE BROTHERS and sisters were all of ordinary size. On page 7 of the masterpiece one finds the memorable harangue that commences: "Cape Bretonians, one and all, remember that Angus MacAskill was our countryman," which sounds like an echo of Brutus over the body of Cæsar. Here it is proudly revealed that the giant "was a native of Cape Breton." On page 13, after some account of Fingal and Ossian, and a short description of the Hebrides based on *J. B. Calkin's Gen. Geography*, we learn further that: "Here [on Lewis, one of the Outer Hebrides] our illustrious hero, Angus MacAskill, was born in the year 1825."

Owing to the inscrutable ways of biology, the infant was at birth abnormally small, sickly, and was not expected to live. After six pages of discussion upon the discovery of America, the state of government in Nova Scotia, and international politics, one reads with a thrill of patriotic pride that Angus attained the age of six years, and was able to accompany his family in their migration to St. Ann's in Cape Breton, where the giant spent the rest of his life with the exception of a protracted interlude of which details will be given in due course. In relation to the voyage itself, there is a touch-

ing scene described, showing the little boy's distress
and subsequent bravery:

> Angus shed tears, too. Next morning the ship left the
> harbour. When Angus realized that they were actually going
> to live out of sight of the old home, he cried bitterly.
>
> However, as was customary, when the vessel proceeded out
> a piece, twelve violinists stood at the stern. Soothed by this
> sprightly air, he pouted "I'll be a man yet, and may yet see my
> own, my native land", and he did see the country of his birth,
> which may be credited to some extent to his determined will.
>
> This may possibly remind some of Napoleon at the Bridge
> of Lodi. 'Twas at the Bridge of Lodi, during an exciting engage-
> ment with the Austrians, that the idea flashed through Napoleon
> Bonaparte's mind that he might yet be a great man.
>
> However, after an otherwise uneventful voyage, Angus Mac-
> Askill arrived safely at St. Ann's, Victoria County, Cape Breton
> Island.

There follows a seven-page description of that part
of the Island made famous by the giant's residence in
it. Here we find the word picture of St. Ann's that in
poetic beauty is unrivalled by any other chapter, except
that devoted to the coffin. But, in an analytic study
like this, I have thought best to arrange the scenery in
a separate section covering backgrounds, and to confine
myself here to MacAskill himself.

When we meet him again he has attained manhood,
and is in full possession of the amazing quantity of flesh
and bone for which he is remembered. Of his child-
hood and youth there is no mention outside of the
facts that his father, who seems to have been a farmer,
taught the boy to plough at a very early age, and at

fourteen "he moved slowly, and had nothing to do with other boys of the same age as long as he had more mature company."

Possibly when his biographer began investigations no one then living remembered our hero as a school-boy, and the scenic interlude is artfully intended to divert the reader's attention from the lack of information. But, since a brother was interviewed by Gillis, it is more likely that this period was uneventful, and the author exercised a wise discretion in passing it over lightly.

Education of some sort the giant certainly obtained, as we learn later of letters he wrote to his relatives when he was away from home. Beyond the climate of Cape Breton, that Gillis asserts to be "exceptionally conducive to the growth of humanity," no reason is given for MacAskill's abnormal size, unless the note on his diet may be so interpreted: "After the age of eight years until he arrived at maturity he always ate a bowl of palatable mixture of cream and oatmeal, sometimes called crowdie, after each meal."

At maturity, MacAskill is pictured as follows:

His height was seven and three-fourths feet. He was three feet and eight inches across the shoulders. The palm of his hand was six inches wide and twelve inches long. One of his boots at least is still extant, and is eighteen inches long. A coat and vest of his are to be seen in Boston, Mass., and the vest can be comfortably buttoned over two good sized men. Though his face was becomingly plump, he was never fat. Touching on his face it is interesting to know that it was positively beardless. Hence he was never obliged to patronize the consolations of the barber's chair except for a hair cut or a shampoo. His eyes were blue and deep set. His voice, though musical, was somewhat hollow, owing to his massive wind organism. The reader may gain a faint idea of his resonant voice by getting a friend to sit in an empty puncheon and speak. He weighed over 500 pounds.[1] He was affable, courteous and friendly. His hospitality was famous. . . . . He frequently visited his friends.

Like all good and great men, he had enemies and opponents, but, as he always trod the path of virtue in addition to his strength, his enemies and opponents never got the upper hand literally, financially or pugilistically, or generally speaking in any way. Yet he never risked the extension of his lines by trying too many things. . . .

Such, such was Angus MacAskill, a man whose size, strength, kindness, virtues, and exploits will be long remembered. In his own realm of greatness he was the Bonnie Charlie, the Wallace, the Bruce, the Napoleon Bonaparte, the Marshall Ney, the Wellington, the Nelson, the O'Connel, the Robert Burns, or the Washington of his countless friends, according as they happened to be impressed by the different phases of his greatness.

Tobacco, which MacAskill began to use about the age of twenty, and intoxicating liquors, which he consumed on occasion in generous quantities, gave his biographer some difficulty. For Gillis is a teetotaller; and besides he was a teacher, having to keep in mind the little ones entrusted to his wisdom; and finally there was the ticklish problem of reconciling the use of

---

[1] A recent remark of Gillis's throws some doubt over this figure as to the actual weight of MacAskill. "I avoid exaggeration and leave out lots that might be written. For a prosaic example, if Mr. Stone weighed 200 lb., I write he weighed at least 150 &c., &c." On that basis, if Gillis had said that MacAskill weighed "at least 500 pounds," we would be warranted in assuming that his actual weight was around 666⅔ pounds. Since Gillis positively says the Giant weighed "more than 500 pounds," it is possible he would have tipped the scales at anything from 700 to 1,000 pounds. As a good-sized moose does not weigh over half a ton, it is unlikely that MacAskill's weight exceeded that figure.

these things, of which the author does not approve, with the conception of the perfect hero that dominates the book, and, indeed, caused Gillis to write it.

The dilemma might have daunted a lesser mind; but our author adroitly satisfies both his passion for truth and his determination to portray a flawless man. So there is a chapter on the evils of tobacco and another on those of liquor. In plan, they are parallel. Both are uncompromising sermons; both admit frankly MacAskill's practice, and furnish him with excuses.

In former years, say, thirty or forty years ago, it was not known that alcoholic liquors were so pernicious. It remained for the present studious, laborious and researching generation to discover the danger. Rum, etc., injures a person morally, physically, mentally and financially. This being admitted, why would any one drink strong drink? The author of this book ventures to answer that question. It is because rum, etc., so to speak, creates cheerfulness and happiness. But, dear reader, this cheerfulness and this happiness are merely counterfeits, yes, merely delusions. . . .

Angus MacAskill took a glass of rum, brandy or whisky occasionally. Did I say glass? Well, 'twas a mistake. He used to drink out of a wooden dish called a tub. The tub would hold three glasses.

But, as already suggested some years ago the evil resultants of alcoholic drinks had not been discovered. This serves as an ample apology for those who drank them. No further apology is needed for any one. . . .

Had our hero been of the present day, we may be sure that he'd be an advocate of total abstinence.

Here the wish was evidently father to the thought. Despite the size of his libations, he seems to have been a moderate drinker, impelled by social instincts; and it is at least possible that if he were now alive he might wish to join his friends at their cups, and that he might again be what Gillis says he was in those far-off days— "no niggard in a liquor store."

Tobacco, while admitted to have valuable medicinal properties when "applied to cuts or snake bites, etc.," is roundly condemned; and MacAskill is exonerated on much the same grounds as for his drinking, along with the further argument that the giant could stand it better than other people. Certainly it is not known to have stunted his growth:

> It would take tobacco half a century to make the least impression on him. Should his supply get exhausted he did not care very much, for he could control his craving till it was convenient to have his order sent.

One shrinks from imagining his capacity to smash furniture had he not been able to control his craving! Because he was a strong man; and the author rests his claim for MacAskill's greatness more on his strength than on his size. In introducing this aspect of our subject, I cannot do better than present, in the author's own words, the ploughing incident, which evidently occurred in the earlier years:

> He and his father were out ploughing one afternoon. A neighbour came around, and in the course of a colloquy with our hero bet ten dollars that the field would not be finished that evening. Our hero put up ten dollars, too, and the neighbour went off till a later hour. Soon, however, one of the horses got sick,

and had to be unyoked for that day, whereupon MacAskill stepped into the horse's place, took hold of the traces, and was fairly more than a match for the remaining horse. He filled the sick horse's place successfully for two hours.

This feat is not without parallel; and I would have my readers in Europe and South America know that Cape Breton has had other stalwart sons, several of whom Gillis courteously mentions by name.

The late Mr. Brussard (Jno. Brussard's father), of Margaree Forks, has had but few equals. One day he hauled a plough by the side of an ox for six hours.

Pacific and kindly by nature, MacAskill used his strength like a true knight errant on behalf of his friends, and particularly those who were in trouble. From the several "exploits" recounted by the author, I choose, because of its brevity, that of how the giant rid the community of a dangerous stranger:

One day at the time when MacAskill's fame was dawning, a renowned fighter put in his appearance. MacAskill soon suspected something, but made no remarks. He entertained the stranger in true Cape Breton style. This reminds one of Roderick Dhu's attitude toward his illustrious guest, James V of Scotland, when they met in the wilds of that "home of the happy." At length the question arose, is this burly stranger going to perpetrate a miniature Glencoe massacre in St. Ann? At length, the suspicious case requested our hero to fight him. MacAskill remonstrated with him, told him that pugilism was an abomination, and fraught with evils many. But the stranger persisted, and charged our hero with cowardice. The latter at last said, "all right, my friend, but let us shake hands." Well, dear reader, they did shake hands. Alas for the stranger, I suppose he "never smiled again." MacAskill squeezed the unfortunate man's hand, which caused the blood to flow freely through the tips of the latter's fingers. This stranger was, of course, more fortunate than Sir Henry de Bohun who tried to assassinate King Robert Bruce at Bannockburn. Yet, it is probable he never thought of his adventure with MacAskill without a sense of shame and fear. However, he retreated hastily from St. Ann, well convinced as Britannia rules the waves, Cape Breton rules the earth in the realm of muscular strength.

At the age of twenty-four MacAskill entered upon the great adventure of his life. I do not refer to his marriage; for he remained a bachelor permanently, and one of the very few criticisms I have to make of the "life" is that the author does not give any reason for his hero's failure to marry. The adventure of Mac-Askill's life was an Odyssey: he travelled. He was offered a contract for five years by a man from New York, who wished to exhibit him for gain during that period. Gillis does not name the man, and I have spent considerable time in research, hoping to clear up this important point. The only clue was the mention of Tom Thumb as a fellow traveller and co-exhibit.

As it is well known that P. T. Barnum managed Tom Thumb, I have gone over the records of Barnum's career to see whether the most illustrious of showmen was not involved. The evidence is not conclusive, but it indicates that Barnum did not act personally, but only through one of his agents. In 1848 he ceased travelling with Tom Thumb, whose tours seem to have been conducted thereafter by Barnum's friend and assistant, Mr. Fordyce Hitchcock. The year 1849 was as momentous for Barnum as it was for MacAskill. During the first part of it he opened a second museum in Philadelphia at the corner of Chestnut and 7th Streets, where he exhibited copies of paintings in the Louvre and "from time to time, my transient novelties in the way of giants, dwarfs, fat boys and other attractions."

By October, Barnum was arranging for Jenny Lind's first American tour, and turned over to Mr. Seth B. Howes sole charge of Barnum's Great Asiatic Caravan, Museum and Menagerie. Though Barnum's autobiography does not contain the name of MacAskill among the giants, his association with Tom Thumb leaves no reasonable doubt about MacAskill's being in Barnum's pay, though the gentleman who hired him, and travelled with him, was certainly not Barnum; and we have no proof that it was either Hitchcock or Howes.

The tour extended through Canada, the United States, Cuba and Europe. Few details of the itinerary are available. That he was a great drawing card is clear from the following quotation, which also indicates his high value as a curio compared, say, to Gay's two-headed colt that might be seen for ten cents.

> He was not accustomed to travel very much about the places at which he and his employer called, at least until the rush to see him was over. Were he to perambulate around, few only would pay a dollar to see him thereafter as one good look at him would satiate curiosity to a bearable extent.

If our interest were centred in MacAskill, we should regret the paucity of the information given about these eventful years of the tour. Since, however, the giant lives because of his biographer no less than Samuel Johnson was immortalized by James Boswell, and since Gillis is more of a creative writer while Boswell was only a glorified reporter, we are happy to endure any loss of information about MacAskill that gives Gillis room for original observations. Thus, as writing, the three-quarters of the chapter on Queen Victoria that enshrines the author's views on the institution of monarchy, and the degree of loyalty a subject owes the Throne, are far more delectable than the account of the giant's interview. However, as we are engaged with MacAskill in this section, the latter will have to be quoted, and the former left to individual research by the many who will wish to purchase the volume.

Be it announced that Her Majesty Queen Victoria invited Angus MacAskill to Windsor Castle. He soon called upon her. She gave him a cordial reception. She chatted pleasantly with him for a few hours.

She was highly *interested* in his great size, and complimented him very warmly. She presented him with two rings of gold.

MacAskill regretted that there was no means of showing his power of lifting,[1] but he thought of a plan to leave a token of his strength on the sly. He walked back and forth before the Queen, secretly pressing the carpet with his heels. When he left, the carpet, though thick and strong, was cut here and there in bread cutter fashion, by the heels of the giant.

The Queen said afterwards that he was the tallest, the stoutest and the strongest man that ever entered the palace.

[1]The Queen was such a small woman that the giant evidently did not think it worth his while to hoist her.

134

What else the Queen said, when she discovered her ruined carpet, may be imagined most accurately by those who know how closely Victoria kept track of her personal possessions.

In Spain MacAskill contracted a severe fever that "lessened his strength over twenty per cent." No date is given for this illness, nor for the incident of the fatal anchor. Walking on a New York pier one evening— some say French sailors taunted him into it—the great man lifted to his shoulder an anchor that was variously estimated to weigh twenty-two hundred or twenty-seven hundred pounds. ("Little did he know 'that soon, too soon', his blooming constitution was going to be blighted forever.") After a short walk, thus encumbered, MacAskill tossed the anchor aside, but one of the flukes caught in his shoulder, crippling him in some mysterious way so that he never fully recovered.

Death, however, was not instantaneous. Supposing he completed his full five years under the contract, and the tragic affair of the anchor was the last thing he did before returning home, he must have survived this mishap by nine years.

On his return to St. Ann, he possessed a "snug fortune"; and he proceeded to establish there two grist mills a prudent distance apart; and happily both "proved very profitable." He also built "an elegant store and stocked it well." His stool, like his ledger, is "still extant," and consists of a 180-gallon molasses puncheon. These years of milling, and store-keeping, and being a celebrity, were happy ones; and thus situated the giant met his death on the 8th August, 1863, at the comparatively early age of thirty-eight. He had been stricken with "that dire ailment, brain fever. The disease set in without any apparent cause."

Now we come to the finest chapter in the book; and because of its chaste beauty I feel compelled to quote it entire. Readers will note the dexterous way in which the author overcomes his ignorance of dimensions, as well as his æsthetic joy over the handles:

CHAPTER XXVIII

THE COFFIN

AFTER OUR HERO'S DEATH, AMONG THE FIRST THINGS CONSIDERED was a coffin. In those times imported coffins were not yet dreamed of. Two reputable carpenters undertook to make the coffin, and they had it completed in six hours.

The coffin was made of native pine boards, as coffins usually were in the days when pine was plentiful. The cover was one-fourth glass.

In size the coffin was a sight of a lifetime. Yet, so well proportioned was it that it looked uncouth by no means. Yes, it seemed to be smaller than what an actual measurement would attest.

It was costly lined with white cloth. Great pains were taken with every detail. Accomplished ladies and gentlemen vied with one another in showing their respect, admiration and appreciation of this extraordinary man.

The exterior of the coffin was lovely. The bright mountings shone out in harmonious contrast with the sober dark ground which they embellished.

In due time the sad task of laying our hero's remains in their last earthly home was becomingly performed. The lid being replaced, the spectators in dozens paced orderly along once more to "gaze on the face that was dead." Bouquets and wreaths without number were brought along. An aged aristocratic man present who had spent years in Edinburgh said "I have seen many a coffin; but, if this is not the costliest coffin I have seen, it is the most beautiful and the best festooned. These bouquets would do honour to a prince. Never have I seen such genuine and sensible indications of sorrow as MacAskill's mourners have evinced."

The minister of the congregation arrived at the appointed hour. After prayer and scriptural reading he preached an appropriate sermon. His Christian and modest eulogy of our hero will long be remembered.

During the sermon many wept. But ere he had neared the end, the mists of sadness began to dissolve "like the dim fabric of a vision", and when the movement of the benediction arrived, there was not a sad heart in the crowd.

But, reverting to the coffin, the reader has probably by this time formed an idea thereof in his or her mind. The beauty of it can be imagined by comparisons or "modern instances." But to imagine its size is very difficult.

It has been said that figures speak. That is a true saying. Yet the actual dimensions of our hero's coffin need not be given, another way of communicating an idea of its size being judged, more easily grasped, and more easily remembered moreover.

Hence, an emphatic illustration is chosen to convey the idea, not at all as a substitute, but as a better medium of this knowledge. Figures may be forgotten, but the following disclosure never.

When the woodwork of the coffin was finished i.e., when it was ready for the dressing, etc., it was found to be sufficient *to bear or float three men across the Bay of St. Ann's.*

The italics, which are his, are approved by the present writer.

Hardly less well turned is Chapter XXIX, *Mac-Askill's Grave.* The following passages from it are self-explanatory; but the author's specially apt choice of words calls for careful study and hearty commendation.

On the eastern side of St. Ann's Bay, about a mile and a half from the sea, there is a bonnie cemetery. As you go down by the bay, facing north, it is on your right hand side. Less than a mile to the south of it, on your left hand side, is one of St. Ann's churches, a magnificent building, with a vane on the top of the spire, which tells the observer there the four fundamental points of a compass, and what's of little less importance "the way the wind blows."

The church referred to above is to aid the stranger in locating the cemetery without asking too many questions. Strangers who are extremely modest like to be spared the odium of asking questions on every side.

In this cemetery the vegetable kingdom is profusely represented. There are elder bushes, cherry trees, raspberry bushes, low wild-rose bushes, and many other beauties of the kind. It reminds one of a passage that we read in Lucy Flemming—that quaint, though happy phrase, "its cheerful graves."

On the upper level of the cemetery, a mound of earth twelve feet in length, artistically set off with gravel, and a respectable gravestone mark the earthly resting place of our hero.

A few feet to the north-east of it are the graves of Mr. and Mrs. Rev. Abraham MacIntosh. Rev. Mr. MacIntosh was pastor of St. Ann's and North Shore. He died on March 10, 1889. His wife's maiden name was Annie Ross. She was born in 1822, and died in 1884. There is a becoming paling yard around their graves. Lastly there's a superb monument, which, if not necessary to perpetuate the memory of their virtues, designates to the tourist their cosy abode at the top of the hill of life which, like John Anderson and his wife, they weel "had climbed together."

The breath of St. Ann's cemetery is as fragrant and sweet as that of a flower garden. As one walks along he is apt to imagine that a costly deodorant has been sprinkled about a few minutes ago.

III.—BACKGROUNDS: THE CAPE BRETON SCENE

ALL WHO HAVE VISITED CAPE BRETON ISLAND UNITE IN praise of its scenic beauties. The poetic soul of James D. Gillis has naturally been stirred by these landscapes; and it is most appropriate that the ablest descriptions of those scenes should have come from the pen of a gifted native son. He is by no means the first eminent author to succeed in making the backgrounds of his narratives as fascinating as the doings of his characters. This rugged country, challenging in its grandeur, inspires him to the composition of many eloquent paragraphs, sustained with a fine gusto, like the swift picture of Upper Margaree:

> Mountains, glens, rocks and valleys, intersected with streams of becoming size; clearances, houses, barns, wood factories and forests—all these are here, as it were in semi-careless profusion.

How real all these places become in his skilful hands! Some biographers have limned their subjects against the political history or social conditions of their times. Gillis does no more of that than is necessary; and instead we see MacAskill moving among the fisher-folk of the villages, or tramping the enchanting roads that lead upward through the pleasant farms, and on into the forests that clothe the hills. Quite the most charming thing in the book is the love that Gillis has for the country of his birth. It, like other things for which we esteem his volume, is a purely unconscious expression of himself. He has the heart of a poet, that Celtic capacity for quick response to beauty in any form, though he prefers it wild. As MacAskill plays his drama, the scene of his "exploits" recurs continually like a *leitmotif*. This aspect is so important that I preferred to treat it in a separate section.

Note, please, how the genius of Gillis by two words has lent personality to the Margaree River:

> From Lake Ainslie flows the South-West of Margaree River, a river, though fairly large, still unassuming, a river whose intrinsic loveliness, coupled with still more charming surroundings, has a prominent place in the directory of superb phenomena.

And, along with the scenery, are the ever courteous country people, who are always giving the author a ride, or supplying him with information, pressing him to stay for a meal, or putting him up for the night, till they also become a minor theme:

> From Upper Margaree to St. Ann's the people along the road are good, always profuse in furnishing information or any other restorative the wayworn may require.

There are some places on this earth where Nature's majesty strikes the beholder with awe. Gillis's *locale* boasts many such, and he does not fail to be impressed:

> Between Egypt and Gilander's Mountain, Middle River, Victoria County, there is a defile through the forest of three

miles' duration. Over this road a buggy will roll and jolt with some safety, barring accidents. Shortly after emerging from the forests, the tourist sights Middle River, upon which he is apt to gaze "long and thoughtfully", as Napoleon Bonaparte gazed on Moscow.

But, fittingly, the most lyrical of his descriptions is saved for MacAskill's old home, the village of St. Ann's by the Bay of the same name. Though it is the longest chapter in the book, and the Giant is not mentioned in it, one can feel that the stage is being set for his entry. How natural that he should wish to return to this beauteous spot after his years in Barnum's museums and travelling shows! The author, too, has loved the place; and one understands and sympathizes with his wish to do it full justice: his evident pride in the sawmill, and in the quality of North River hay, do him credit. These specimen paragraphs not only bring this pleasant rural scene vividly before the eye, but also illustrate at its best Gillis's deftness in the choice and arrangement of words.

At the mouth of St. Ann's Bay, on the west side is the town, Englishtown. The people of Englishtown are remarkably progressive. Education receives due attention.

Scores of sailing and steaming vessels plough the waters of St. Ann's every week. As these gigantic cradles gently rock, they resemble fabulous vultures of the deep in the act of sunning themselves and resting moreover before taking one of their long and happy flights.

There is a sufficiency of wharves. Not far from one of these is a saw-mill which would be no disgrace to a lumber company in New Brunswick.

Into the west side of St. Ann's Bay rolls the lordly North River. This river flows through a fertile region. Yes, the farmers of North River need but "tickle the ground, and it smiles with a harvest." Again, North River hay, pressed or otherwise, has more than local reputation.

The chief occupations of St. Ann's people are farming, fishing, navigating and lumbering. Farming heads the list in lucrative importance, the others follow as above respectively in order of descending magnitude of profit.

The homes of St. Ann's might remind the tourist of Mrs. Heman's poetical tribute to the lovely "homes of England." The exterior of these (the former) are only excelled by their interiors. Clumps of flowery flower-plants are seen in discreet profusion mildly blooming outside the inviting open doors of these palatial cottages, as if the florid sources of varied sweetnesses within "had run o'er", as the gold of Venice seemed, to Rogers, yes, "had run o'er", which necessitated the removal of the plant inhabitants outside the music resounding walls.

In surroundings such as these, where "cows and calves add a lustre to their allotted villas," it is natural for MacAskill to have expanded physically, and for Gillis to have found inspiration for his poetic prose.

IV.—THE SAYINGS OF A SAGE

POWERFUL MINDS OFTEN HAVE THE FACULTY OF SHOWING that a subject has more sides than would ordinarily be suspected, and of commenting illuminatingly on matters outside the strict limits of their themes. Thus it has been said of Emerson that one may transpose sentences and whole paragraphs from one part of an essay to another, and even from one essay to another, without spoiling his argument. Or, if we removed from Shakespeare's plays all the characters' wise and witty remarks that do not forward the plot to its conclusion, the continuity of the stories would not suffer, but our loss would be incalculable. So *obiter dicta* have come to occupy a place of honour; and it may be that in them an author has his greatest chances of immortality.

So, with fullest respect to the able manner in which he has done MacAskill's life, Gillis's reflections and comments upon life in general save the book from being merely a biography, and make it what it is. The man—to put it bluntly—is much bigger than his set subject, large as that undoubtedly was. It is everywhere apparent that he needed more scope. That is why we find him inserting opinions that do not belong in the conventional biography. Far from blaming him, I am happy (and I am sure I speak for all his readers) that he was bold enough to defy convention, and refuse to bow to the "foolish consistency" that Emerson labelled "the hob-goblin of little minds."

Nor is any account of his masterpiece adequate that omits mention of the many examples of his stepping outside his subject to give intellectual leadership, where he thinks necessary in the public interest. "Can medical science account for all the causes of freckles?" he enquires, and plunges into a dissertation on the pigmentation of the human skin that would have opened the eyes of Sir William Osler. Therefore I have added this brief section on Gillis's miscellaneous wisdom; but to confine the appreciation within reasonable limits I have decided to deal only with the political and philosophic *obiter dicta,* and to furnish only three examples of each.

Politically, he has grasped the great principle that loyalty should begin at home, and he espouses fearlessly an uncompromising creed of home rule for Cape Breton:

> While a military government would not be adequate today, it is clear it would be much better for the island to be still, and forever, a separate province. With due respect to the inhabitants of the peninsula, we are satisfied that it adds nothing to our dignity at home or abroad to be affiliated with them under one provincial Government. As for roads and bridge grants, etc., there is a "leagued oppression" against Cape Breton in these matters, which needs no Argus to observe. However, there is a

sentiment among the islanders in favour of secession. At a seasonable opportunity a "long, strong pull together" will gain for us that separation which will be the keystone to our political freedom.

Immigration being now a most important problem for all Canada, his remarks of fifty years ago are still timely:

> When MacAskill was a youth, the subject of immigration to America was pervaded with great and sometimes unrealized expectations. Of course, truth is stranger than fiction, and a truthful account of America could not be exceeded in wonders and interest by the most fabulous orator. Yet, there is not a clime on earth where all succeed. Even America is not an exception, though it offers the poor exceptional chances. Hence it was that many immigrants even from Scotland were disappointed.

His hostility to the neighbouring republic is seen in his frank rejoicing over "the collapse of United States trade" in St. Ann's Bay due to a Dominion Government regulation requiring foreign fishermen to obtain licenses before buying bait from the natives. Elsewhere, he issues the general warning:

> The people of the United States, generally speaking, love their country and their countrymen to a remarkable degree. This is not unreasonable, for their country is a great one, and they have and have had their great men. But some Americans go so far as to ignore the idea that there are countries and men in other longitudes and latitudes as great as theirs.
>
> The above remark is intended to warn the reader to be cautious in weighing the patriotic effusions of our friends "over

the border." Let the Canadian study neutral statistics, and then decide for himself about the comparative greatness of the United States.

That is delicately put.

Philosophy is the art of co-relating sciences. Science seeks facts, and within a limited field joins fact to fact to formulate laws; but it remains for philosophy, surveying the whole activity of man, to reconcile the findings of the different sciences, and adduce broader statements on the nature of man and the universe, and to determine the direction, if not the goal, of life. Science is knowledge, philosophy is understanding. How philosophy clarifies and makes of practical use the abstract data supplied by science is illustrated neatly in the paragraph on heredity, a subject still dangerous for the scientists themselves. Note, then, the firm grasp of its essentials by Gillis:

A few remarks on heredity may not be inappropriate. Nature works in mysterious ways. A child may bear a striking facial resemblance to his father, while his limbs may resemble those of his maternal grandfather. Again a *man* may not resemble his father a visible iota, and his son may be the picture of his parental grandfather. But in the case of such a man the points of resemblance were there, though not evinced. Moreover, a man may be found to be almost a duplicate of a great grand uncle. Yet, as a rule, and as a rule a salutary thing it is, children are the ideal images of their parents. And though "Auld Nature" wantonly as if by accident deviates occasionally from her rule far enough to use anew the moulds in which our remote ancestors were moulded, it rather strengthens than weakens the belief that

146

Nature intended us all to be and to look a little or more like one another, and like Adam and Eve. This phenomenon of Nature is called heredity.

The discourse on unanimity is an example of philosophy at work in the domain of politics, one of the major diversions in the activities of organized mankind. Here we have the profundity of a Spinoza united with the lightning-swift changes of direction of thought of a Lloyd George. Gillis here escapes the ancient charge of Omar Khayyam against philosophy that it leads the seeker out by the same door through which he entered. There are two doors to Gillis's House of Reason, and as he passes out the back door, he slams it after him with italics to emphasize that his cogitations have got him somewhere:

The absence of unanimity has retarded the progress of nations. It had something to do with the failure of Charles Edward Stuart (Bonnie Prince Charlie). Yes, dissensions retarded the progress of Scotland, Ireland and of England. Even in our great Dominion of Canada, dissensions, political and otherwise, have sometimes proved very embarrassing.

Not so in the island of Cape Breton. What dissensions we have had owed their origin to varied opinions respecting the means to be employed for certain praiseworthy ends. As all parties were sincere, and meant to do good, and did good, these superficial tempests were almost essential constituents of unanimity.

A discreet quantity of word warring strengthens the right. The difficulty is to gauge ourselves at the proper line. The philosophy of the benefits of opposition suggested in the preceding sentences is something that only one in two thousand have learned.

Those who have not time to study large books on this philosophy can proceed in another way. Let them watch and observe discussions. As a rule they will find that the results where all thought and spoke alike *are always weak*.

Fishing, the contemplative art, is well adapted to exemplify the practical value of meditation, which is the supreme contribution of Oriental philosophy. And it is a happy circumstance that a philosopher closely allied to the fishing industry should have been the one to point out the soul development possible peculiarly to the fisherman through this philosophic exercise:

Fish and fishing illustrate or illustrate more and better morals than Æsop's fables. The credulity of some fishes, shows the folly of extreme credulity. The imperative painstaking of the fisherman proves the necessity of taking pains in what is to be done before success may be expected. If the reader be a keen observer and thinker, and a person of force, he or she may derive pleasure, recreation and benefit, from a thorough consideration of fish and fishing. But a warning note may not be amiss. It is dangerous to think too much on such matters—half an hour in the afternoon is sufficient.

What more appropriate situation in which to leave our real hero, who is Gillis, than in profound contemplation of "the credulity of some fishes"? I admit it is with some envy that I leave him thus engaged; for in the much fished waters of southern Ontario I have often been quite unphilosophically annoyed at the extreme wariness and wisdom of some other fishes. This, of course, does not detract from the truth of his assertion, but rather proves it in obverse; and possibly it takes even more philosophy to draw moral lessons from incredulous fishes that do not take the bait; and certainly, as hour follows hour without a bite, the disappointed fisher-philosopher has more time for his meditation—sometimes too long, for has not Gillis warned us against the dangers of indulging for more than a half-hour at a time?

But the "pleasure, recreation and benefit" of reading *The Cape Breton Giant* far outweighs the reflections induced by the "most fabulous" fishes; and now finally, humbly, but very earnestly, I commend the book to the attention of every "keen thinker and observer, and person of force." As its author has well said: "It will be found more interesting than a fairy tale."

* * * * *

After publication of the first edition of this book in 1927, a group of poets called The Song Fishermen, under the inspiration of Robert Norwood, motored to Cape Breton to visit Mr. Gillis at his home. In 1930, he became their guest on a sea cruise. Landing at East Dover, the party had a picnic and poetry contest on a subject taken from The Cape Breton Giant when Mr. Gillis acted as judge.

As a retired school teacher, he realized his ambition of making a journey to Palestine.

In March, 1945, Mr. Gillis spent a week in Halifax as the guest of Andrew D. Merkel and other literary friends. The celebrity delivered a number of public addresses, which were well received. At social gatherings he entertained generously with selections on his bagpipes and violin. He was interviewed on the radio two or three times by Thomas H. Raddall, who was successful in obtaining recordings of several ancient Gaelic songs, which had been brought over by the Highlanders migrating after the rebellion of 1745.

Now, aged 83, Mr. Gillis is still living at Melrose Hill, Cape Breton, where he is enjoying an old age which, happily, promises to be long. In years, he is Canada's senior poet and, in all respects, unique.

James MacRae:
The Man From Glengarry

INVOCATION TO ST. RAPHAEL

Guide of wanderers who seek thy light and aid, do not refuse
Over stormy seas but dimly known to guide my wand'ring muse,
As I strive to scale Parnassus, on its dizzy heights to roam.

MACRAE'S VOLUNTARY ENTRY INTO THE IMMORTAL
ranks of the Jameses was clearly Providential: he was
named otherwise at birth. It is not the first time that
a writer's intuition has helped him to a *nom de plume*
that his readers have felt to be his heaven-ordained
designation. François (or French) Villon was baptised
François, but his original surname was de Montcorbier:
in changing the one, he knew better than to tamper
with the other. François Rabelais was content with the
name given him; but Jacques Anatole Thibault was
moved to change his name to France long before it was
apparent that he was to be the peculiarly French author
of his generation. When Jock MacDonald was moved
to adopt his second Christian name as his pen name, it
was with no thought that the name James would be

one of the qualifications for his occupancy of the fourth place in the famous Canadian quartette. His choice of his mother's family name is less important.

John J. MacDonald, or James MacRae as I shall henceforth call him, was born in 1849 on a farm in Glengarry County, Ontario, just east of the village of Alexandria. He was born to Scottish Roman Catholic parents, his father having come to Canada from Glengarry, Scotland, and his mother from Kintail.

As the son of a pioneer his educational opportunities were meagre, but he managed to obtain three or four years' instruction at the near-by public school. Until the age of twenty he lived on the farm on which he had been born, and then found employment as a labourer for two years on the Grenville Canal. In 1873 he took up the study of engineering, and sat for a preliminary examination for a surveyor's certificate, after which he practiced surveying for two years. In 1875 he moved to St. Mary's, Ontario, and worked a farm near the town—probably on some kind of rental basis, possibly on a share-of-crop lease.

After getting nicely settled in his new environment, he realized his long-cherished ambition of publishing a book. This was a collection of verses entitled *Poems by J. J. MacDonald—A Native of County Glengarry*. Into this modest little volume, the young man of twenty-eight put a large number of short poems on a wide variety of subjects. Best of them, in every way, is the poem to his father's homeland, which the Canadian son claims as his own. The lines have deep feeling; and it is a particular pleasure to quote some of them because MacRae here expresses sentiments shared by the majority of Scottish-Canadians:

THE HIGHLAND RACE

Although I never yet have trod
Sweet Scotland's heath or sacred sod,
I read her children's deeds abroad;
    Their fame is spread
Wherever by the will of God
    Their steps are led.

In foreign lands, to hardships steeled,
For honour's cause the sword they wield
Upon the bloody battle field,
    And win renown;
Before their valor tyrants yield,
    And arms lay down.

Among the ranks of high and low
Their energetic powers they show;
In climes where torrid breezes blow
    They govern there,
Where the St. Lawrence's waters flow,
    And everywhere.

On distant shores while they sojourn,
Their absence from their home to mourn,
Their souls with love for it still burn,
    And oft the while
In leisure moments they'll return
    To range that isle.

Where Scottish kings made Scotland's laws,
Where Wallace fought for freedom's cause,
Will roving fancy love to pause
    On scenes so dear,
Till fond remembrance often draws
    The melting tear.

Where Bruce the gallant people freed,
And where their faithful sons did bleed
For conscience sake, for faith and creed,
    Each fancy strays,
Till they their country's praise proceed
    To sing in lays.

The gifted young farmer was too eligible to remain long a bachelor; and in 1879 he married a girl of pure Irish blood, Bridget Louisa McDonald by name.

MacRae continued with the first farm for ten years until, in 1885, he secured the farm on which he lived for thirty-two years. In 1918, being almost seventy years of age, he retired, and took up his residence in the town of St. Mary's, where he spent a pleasant old age, and where the Public Library was an unfailing source of enjoyment. His mind was active, and he preferred reading books on controversial subjects, like political economy and religion; and often gave the results of his thought to the public in the form of letters to the press. These letters appeared in the St. Mary's *Journal-Argus,* in the London *Free Press,* and in the Toronto *Globe.*

Among the townspeople he was reported to be mildly eccentric, which probably means nothing more than a

strongly marked personality intensified by a touch of
the artistic temperament, without which no poet is
properly equipped. Any one familiar with the history
of literature will remember innumerable manifestations
of the absent-mindedness of great writers; and will not
be surprised to learn that in MacRae this trait took the
form of talking to himself, after he had become so
thoroughly absorbed in his topic as to have forgotten
his surroundings. I like to picture him as he has been
described to me—sitting in the Library, lost in his book,
and, as the theme gripped him, conducting audibly an
animated debate with himself, and finally becoming
quite excited as the argument progressed.

But there is no precedent in all literature for the
hiatus between this author's first and second books.
A. E. Housman is supposed to have set a record by
allowing twenty-five years to elapse between *A Shrop-
shire Lad* and *Last Poems*. Whoever thinks so has
certainly never heard of James MacRae, to whom
belongs the honour of a silence of forty-six years
between the *Poems* of his youth and *An Ideal Courtship*, which was first published in 1923.

This *magnum opus*, composed in the first five years
after retirement from active farm work, is a narrative
poem, in the ballad style of Sir Walter Scott's romances,
running to seven hundred lines. It is a rural Canadian
love story, and notable as the longest and best sustained

flight made by any poet coming within the scope of
this series of studies. Gillis's *The Great Election,* it is
true, is about the same length; but that work is in many
meters, and some of the parts—for instance the love
lyrics—are really independent poems inserted in the
main work. MacRae has only one such—the lament
sung by William at his darling's grave, which has been
taken entire from the *Poems* of 1877. The rest of his
poem is "all of a piece." The same verse pattern is
employed throughout; and while Gillis enlarges on
different topics so much that one may be momentarily
forgetful of the principal theme, MacRae sticks to his
story.

That is not said in disparagement of either man or
method: it is just drawing a distinction. Nor must it
be thought that MacRae's poem is all plot, or uniform
in mood. On the contrary he interprets his characters
as well as delineates them, and draws lessons from his
tale as it proceeds. So full, indeed, is it of his own
interesting personality, that some doubt exists as to its
purport. When reviewing the book on its appearance,
I was under the impression that the author's principal
aim was to write a moral tract in the palatable form of
a story, embellished with the poet's art. Consequently
I referred to the book as "an antidote to lascivious
novels, treatises on birth control, and the evils of mixed
marriages." I have since learned that his intention

was not the implanting of ideals in the minds of young
Canadians, but "to laud the Scotch." His goal as
expressed in the poem, however, is quite definite:

Let me find the cause most fruitful of the sins of married folk,
Of the miseries and troubles that make rough their galling yoke
That with this my rambling story I may finally succeed
In prescribing for their benefit the remedy they need.

In their careless preparation for their holy state we find
That the votaries of Hymen are rash, negligent and blind;[1]
That their motives for embracing it unworthy are and base;

* * * *

In their rash and thoughtless folly, down the cup of love they
    drain,
Nothing for the years that follow but the bitter dregs remain.

* * * *

Ah! did lovers for their unions but prepare one half as well
As do other men and women for the altar or the cell.

The proper end of marriage, every man should
know, is:

Not to gratify his passions but to propagate his kind.

This is not the first time that an author has done
something he did not originally intend, nor that a
public has chosen to adapt a book to its own needs.
Swift's *Gulliver's Travels*, meant as a bitter political
satire, owes its long life to its use as a fairy story for

---

[1]Compare Gillis's opinion on page 107 in the passage commencing: "The
mutual love of either sex."

children. But if MacRae did not consciously intend to preach, his mind, like Bernard Shaw's, runs to moral problems so much that his poem is as much a sermon as it is a story.

MacRae is a conservative in social theory as he is in politics. An intelligent, not a bigoted one. He adduces good reasons for doubting the value of the commonly vaunted "modern progress," and for preferring the simpler life of an earlier day:

Though the people then were forced to live upon a poorer hearth,
And knew nothing of biology or of control of birth,
Or what modernists are teaching for improvement of the race,
Whose immoral artificial means, the natural replace.

More general observations and specimens of wisdom are scattered generously throughout the narrative. Instinctively, he sympathizes with the poor:

Oft the poor who trust in Heaven up the ladder lightly go,
While the rich who look down proudly tumble headlong down below.[1]

* * * *

Man cannot be wisely trusted but with limited supplies.
To the path that leads to suicide he is inclined to stray,
When he finds that he can do it in an easy, pleasant way.

An interesting example of the attitude of the conservative to change in fashions is found by comparing MacRae's strictures on women's costumes in 1923 with

---

[1]Compare Gay: *"O! What will be the rich man's fate?*
Too late! too late, too late" (page 36).

his complaints of 1877. Now, of course, he rebukes women scathingly for wearing too little; but fifty years ago he was equally shocked that they wore so much—pads and multitudinous draperies that concealed the female form in a way God had never intended. The complete covering of the body he calls dishonest, since by it men were prevented from seeing the bodily defects of the women, and might be sadly undeceived after marriage:

> How oft thus lay the secret way
> In which the game is played:—
> A shapeless mass, by name a lass,
> Is artfully arrayed,
> Is neatly bound with metal round
> And trimmings wisely made,
> And padded o'er with worthless store
> To cover unbetrayed
> The sad defects, which one detects
> When nature is displayed.

It appears (a fact wholly new to me, and that is why I interject it here) that this surplusage of clothing of the late seventies was placed strategically at such points as not to hide whatever attractions of form the ladies possessed:

> With tender care they leave quite bare
> What parts are fit to face,
> Or please the eyes of youths they prize,
> No matter what their place.

The story with its inspiring example, may be outlined without further prelude; and the quotations will enable the reader to appreciate the quality of the poetry. The scene is the banks of the River Garry in Eastern Ontario. The heroine, who was one of a family of twelve children, is called Mary Campbell—

Mary was the youngest of them, so she was her parents' pet,
And the best of care and training they determined she would get,
But apart from worldly comforts their design and chief desire
Was to form her as a model for the public to admire.

She was not to be a mannikin, but was sent to public school, and later to a convent, in order to acquire both earthly and heavenly wisdom:

The non-Christian to prepare her for a prosperous career,
And the convent as auxiliary to polish or veneer.

The father, who seems to have been an amateur theologian of ability, supplemented the catechism and confirmation instruction by reasoning out with Mary many abstruse points, such as:

And if Lazarus was married when his shortened death he died,
When he rose would it be right for him to take another bride?
And as to his former partner, would she still have to remain
A dejected, lonely widow till he married her again?

It was when Mary was undergoing the final part of her education at the convent that she experienced calf-love with Robert Fraser, who attended the adjacent Brothers' school. Communication was established by notes through the fence, and an old-fashioned private post-office—an institution that I fear has fallen into disuse along with the game of the same name. Mary took this affair very seriously:

Though her lips did not reveal them, he could easily surmise
All the depth of her affections in her rolling, starry eyes.

Callously, with his eye to material advancement, he left her for another:

She was sorely disappointed, she was stunned but did not fall,
Struck upon the rawest spot, though not so hard as was St. Paul.

In her sorrow and humiliation, there returned to her mind the precepts in morals and piety she had learned at the convent:

Some recesses still retained them, and like beast of bovine blood,
In her silent, lonely leisure, she had time to chew the cud.

The authentic hero, William Chisholm, was a native of the Maritime Provinces; and the poet's knowledge of his history is artfully explained by the claim that William's diary is in the poet's possession:

So if any of my readers to believe it should refuse,
I myself or else my heirs can this old diary produce.

William was the right sort of fellow. He knew the purpose of marriage; and was too wise to marry a girl for her money. As a lover, he seems to have been a little stolid, objecting to face powder, and to girls who were fond of dances, or who dressed immodestly. Of a studious cast, he was disgusted with the number of frivolous books he found:

In the literature current in our libraries and press
He could find but little wheat by delving mountain piles of chess.[1]

It would take too long to tell of all the things in this world William disapproved; but that he was conscious of a certain sourness in his nature is evident from the assertion that he relied on the law of attraction of opposites to bring him a good-natured wife:

> . . . it is opposites attract.
> William was assured by this that with his destined wife he'd find
> Many amiable qualities of body and of mind.

His book knowledge had been supplemented by a sad experience. For he, too, like Mary, had had a disappointing love affair; and this may have had something to do with his misanthropy.

One fair maiden near him William would have chosen for his
   bride,
But when asked, she in the negative disdainfully replied.
He and his connections were the leading farmers of the place,
While the sum of her endowments was her muscle, heart and
   face.

While I admire William probably as much as MacRae meant every one to admire him, I confess that I do not like him sufficiently to be deeply affected by his misfortune. My sympathies are all with the unnamed

[1] A common noxious weed.

162

girl who rejected him. The poet is possibly sarcastic about the damsel's merits, when compared to William's; but surely her "endowments" of "muscle, heart and face" made her a most desirable bride for a young farmer, and if William had not been quite so conscious of his own high station, perhaps he might have had her. But then this story would never have been written, because it was his grief, or more likely hurt pride, that drove William west to Glengarry, where Mary awaited him. It is to be hoped she was grateful to the other girl for taking a little of William's conceit out of him.

The actual falling in love of William and Mary is somewhat blurred by an extended homily against long courtships, reading in part, as follows:

Close acquaintance breeds contempt for those we know so much
    about,
And exposes prematurely what must finally leak out.
This applies especially to lovers, and I would direct
Them to note that lengthy courtships have this specified effect.

On the other hand, four lines further on, we find there are also dangers in not knowing exactly what one may find in a mate. In other words, it is better to know before it is too late "what must finally leak out."

Ladies leaving those they know of for the strangers they admire
Often jump out of the heated frying-pan into the fire.

Having prepared everything, the poet is now unfortunately stricken with doubts about his powers to

describe the details of the wooing, which is a great pity.
This should have been the *denouement* of the drama.
The poet offers his excuse in well turned lines:

And I could not well describe it even if I so desired,
For my muses' flight has been so long, her weakly wings are tired,
So she dare not any energy extravagantly spend,
But meagerly distribute it and stretch it to the end.

That end is now in sight, hastened possibly by the
failing wings of the poet's muse. William's father dies
conveniently, and the young man's inheritance allows
the happy pair to become formally engaged, and to
prepare for marriage.

At the scene of their engagement no rash liberties took place,
Nor did he attempt to seal it with a kiss or an embrace.

There had been a moment of uncertainty, when
William had cautiously come to the point of being sure
he wanted to marry Mary, and realized that his finances
were insufficient. It was then that he reconciled himself to going away to work, and to depending on the
mails to carry on his sedate love making:

And to keep up correspondence with his darling he would then
Have to change his vocal organs for the mailbag and the pen.

The inherited money prevented the separation:

The receipt of William's legacy enabled him and her
To prepare to reach their goal and meet expenses to incur.

They did not reach it after all; and one is not prepared for the suddenness of the calamity that follows

the decorous engagement. Consequently the blow falls
with the greater dramatic force:

Mary suddenly took sick, and human skill could no relief
Render her in her distress, which made the tragic struggle brief.

* * * * * * *

So they laid her in God's acre, but it happened then and there,
That He had not quite an acre, for the measurement was spare.[1]
The good people would have given Him a larger piece of ground,
For they had it in abundance in the neighbourhood around;
But they were so clannish that they wanted very little room
And preferred to snuggle tight together even in the tomb.

William, distraught, lost his mind, and spent most
of his time in the cemetery:

While on earth he stayed so faithful to her mortal body nigh,
Soared his spirit up in fancy to her dwelling-place on high.

At the grave, Ophelia-like, he sang:

Every breeze around me that goes whistling by
Draws another bubble from my tearful eye.

After days of absence, he is sought for and found:

And though all around is withered, yet they tell it who have seen
That the grass above her bosom with his tears is growing green.
Acting on the few suggestions that the said informant gave,
They proceeded till they found him, kneeling on his darling's
grave.

Grief, damp exposure, and lack of food had done for
William, who died, a little theatrically, at the very day

---

[1] It will be remembered that the poet had been a surveyor.

and hour set for the wedding. The poem concludes
with the celestial re-union:

Though so often disappointed by events beyond their power,
They were finally united at their own appointed hour.
But so well their lives were ended, and so holy was their love,
We may hope that they were married at the altar steps above.
If ye lovers tell the story, be the burden of your prayers:
"May our motives be as worthy and our love as pure as theirs."

When a reviewer had the temerity to suggest that
there is Biblical assurance of there being neither marry-
ing nor giving in marriage in heaven, the poet replied
with a sheaf of references to support his claim. It is
a point Mary's father would have liked to reason out,
possibly in debate with the poet himself. I do not
presume to contest the point; but must call attention
to MacRae's contrary opinion as set forth in his earlier
book:

Dear reader, please in mind to bear,
That in the realms of bliss above,
There is no wife permitted there
To man, however strong his love.

In any case, the very sad ending of the poem can
hardly be an encouragement to young people to emulate
the pure love of William and Mary. Their noble re-
nunciation may appeal to those who have been long
married; but few young men of today would look
forward eagerly to having their best girls die before the
wedding, to say nothing of actually praying that it
might be so.

That is the human side. From a literary standpoint, the "grand style" has been maintained throughout. Thought and diction are alike lofty; the rhyming is perfect; and the greatest care has been taken to have the right number of syllables in every line.

During the four years that have elapsed since publication of *An Ideal Courtship*, MacRae has completed another lengthy narrative in verse. This appears in the *Complete Poems* of 1930.

The Ladies: God Bless Them!

> Little one, thou art sweeter far
> Than any petal textured star,
> Sweeter than a lover's gift,
> Thou art joy that God hath whiffed!
> —*Lady Roddick.*

IN THE CASE OF ONLY ONE OF THE WRITERS, WHOSE works have been considered in this volume, was poetic genius transmitted to an offspring. James McIntyre's daughter, and only surviving child, inherited something of her sire's ability as a poet. Kate (McIntyre) Ruttan is a widow of Lavallee, Ontario, in the Rainy River district. Her book, *Rhymes Right or Wrong of Rainy River*, was published in 1926. From which I have already quoted both poems in praise of her father, the "Caledonian Bard." Her muse is intent on local themes to an extent that forbids copious quotation here. The following lines to a Presbyterian minister may be taken as typical of her more serious work:

REVEREND LAVIS

> Three cheers for Lavis,
> He sings like a mavis,
> Preaches like Paul,
> Like Apollo does water,
> Demands a revival,
> And of good the survival,
> Oh, happy the clay
> In the hands of this potter.

THE LADIES: GOD BLESS THEM!

ANASTASIA HOGAN, AT THE TIME OF HER EARLY ACTIVITY
in the eighteen-nineties, was a resident of Newfoundland. She is presumably of Irish descent. Her melodies
are clearly traceable to Tom Moore as inspirational
source, rather than to Robbie Burns. Like all good
children of Erin, she loved the home of her race, and
its floral emblem:

THE SHAMROCK

'Tis small, but represents that Isle,
That's famous for abundant soil,
Those leaves are dear to Irish hearts,
They shall never die till life departs

Her book, *Poems,* published in Newfoundland, also
speaks generously of that country. She was very fond
of its scenery; and one landscape is very beautifully
described in the stanzas *To Quidi Vidi River*:

O'er earth a prettier scenery
Is very rarely found,
In a valley lie thy waters deep,
On each side a burying ground.

The coming and going of the ships delighted her.
There are references to buoys, lighthouses, and ship-
wrecks. The poem to the oil tanker *Rotterdam* expresses
her joy over the averting of a marine disaster:

Our harbour now is this ship's home,
Saved from the surging threat'ing foam.
Good luck has guided her off the rock,
And gave her a chance to try our dock.

169

For all that, Anastasia Hogan would not have been a disciple of Moore unless sentimental topics had engaged her more than any others. And this is the case. She is the poet of the tender passion. The titles are enough to indicate how often her heart had been quickened, and sometimes hurt: *Parted, To an Old Photograph, To a Lock of Hair, To an Absent One, To S——, To G——, Parted* (a second time), *Blue Eyes, Black Eyes, Parted* (third episode), *Thoughts on H——,* and so on. Anastasia appears to have loved easily and often. Among them all, *and very properly too,* it is *Blue Eyes* that contains her most famous quatrain:

> I revel in those beauteous eyes,
> Time passes by while gazing on them,
> Oh, happy hours absorbing flies,
> Life is naught to me without them.

It is only fair to the poet's reputation to add that some—a minority—prefer the opening stanzas of *First Dream of Love.* In this matter I am no heretic. I stand with the majority in believing *Blue Eyes* to be the more remarkable performance, while ready to concede that *First Dream* also has merit, though of a lesser order, and am more than willing to quote both that my readers may make their free choice between the two:

FIRST DREAM OF LOVE

> As I think and look back on years that are past,
> And see the great changes take place,
> The first dream of love thro' all years will last,
> To the end of all human race.

170

THE LADIES: GOD BLESS THEM!

The bright, loving tales, the happy gay hours,
The sweet, winsome smile that she gave,
My life to me then was as sweet as the flowers,
Bedewed by youths rivulets lave.

THE CANADIAN WEST IS REPRESENTED BY LILLIAN FORBES
Gunter, whose *Loving Memories and Other Poems* was
published at Regina about 1923. I have been able to
gather no other information about her, except that she
personally took orders in Regina for her book, and has
not been seen there since its publication. She has
evidently had some experience on a homestead, as her
Reverie is an exceptionally faithful picture of a
bachelor's life on the prairie.

THE BACHELOR'S REVERIE

A bachelor, young and handsome,
Sat musing one day in his shack,
Way out on the western prairie,
Where girls are the things that they lack:
This bachelor sat and soliloquized,
As bachelors oft' have to do,
Says he, "My, don't I wish I were married,
This thing is sure driving me blue;
No one to smile a glad welcome,
No one to kiss me good-bye,
If I step to the well for some water,
Or with swill make a trip to the sty;
No one to get me my breakfast,
No one to kindle the fire,
And when I'm detained at the lodge room
There's no one the cause to inquire;
No one to yank out my whiskers,
No one to climb on my knee,

And no one to handle the broomstick,
Should I get on a bit of a spree;
No one to get me up early,
No one to keep me up late,
No one to praise or to scold me,
No one to love or to hate.
But here! I must wash up these dishes,
Great Scott! can that be a plate?
And there is that rag of a dishcloth
On the bed-post, serenely sedate,
Now I must sweep up this mansion,
Though the naughty microbes may demur,
And finish my model housekeeping
By giving the blankets a stir,
I'm glad Mrs. Smith does my baking,
My! if I had a woman like her,
But, see here, young fellow, don't covet,
Be a man but don't be a cur."

Journalistic Prose in Newfoundland

IT IS ALWAYS A DIFFICULT MATTER TO SAY HOW FAR stylists like Gillis and Carlyle are indebted to common countryside speech for their striking idioms, and how far they, in their turn, impose their own twists of phrase upon their contemporaries. Some of James D. Gillis's expressions, we know, have gained wide currency in the Maritime Provinces. Of that, others can write with more authority than I. During recent years it has been my privilege to be enabled to make certain comparisons of his diction with that used in the newspapers of our sister Dominion; and the following is intended to exemplify many delightful word usages common to them and to the Cape Bretonian author.

The likenesses may be due, as I have hinted, to a common source, or to the direct influence of Gillis upon journalists on the other side of the Gulf of St. Lawrence. Newspaper writers are quick to pick up forceful or picturesque bits of phraseology. What is specially interesting in the examples of Newfoundland prose I am going to quote, and has a direct bearing on the problem, is that two of the writers—the correspondents from Codroy—are also Gillises, and possibly, like

James D., descendants of "the fertile Angus Gillis" of the poem. Another writer, also from Codroy, who uses the initials "E.D.G.," is almost certainly Edwin D. Gillis, the author of the Hospital article. Almost half the examples to be quoted, therefore, were written by Newfoundland Gillises, who are sure to be familiar with the writings of James D., who is likely a distant relative.

Letters to newspapers, it should be explained, take a much more prominent part in Newfoundland journalism than in Canadian. In Canada, they are printed in small type, and tucked away in inconspicuous corners. In Newfoundland, they appear under display heads, frequently on the front page; and are treated in every respect as the important "news stories" or "interviews" that they really are. So in Newfoundland authorship of such "letters" is the equivalent of authorship of magazine articles—above, not below, the ordinary news columns in literary importance.

The facts respecting *A Dual Tragedy* are that the St. John's *Daily News* had a correspondent at Catalina; that for a long time nothing of importance happened; and then, within half a day, there were two suicides in the place. The local reporter rose to the occasion. Unfortunately the editor was like most other editors, he thought the piece much too long, and put nine-tenths of it in the waste-basket, to the great loss of literature. What was left appeared in the *Daily News* about June 1, 1924. Observe the delicate omission of all names from the account.

A DUAL TRAGEDY

A WOMAN AND A MAN COMMIT SUICIDE, WITHIN A FEW HOURS OF EACH OTHER, AT CATALINA

Early upon the morning of Thursday, the 22nd inst., the inhabitants of this settlement received a very severe shock by the sudden and unexpected announcement that early upon the morning of that day a woman achieved, by drowning, her own destruction. In the main the details are as follows: During the previous night she had slept with two of her children, who upon awakening were startled upon finding that mother was not in the bed with them. A search for her in the house proved futile, the alarm that she was missing was raised which resulted in the discovery of a sweater dropped in the doorway of the house from which she had made her perilous and final flight. Eventually she was traced and discovered by some section employees upon the railway at a little distance from where they were working, or at the "steadies," a brook crossed, when frozen in the winter, by the woodsmen. It is a comparatively short distance North of the settlement, en route to the woods. In the effort to circumvent her intention, when she realized that she had been discovered and that a strenuous preventive effort was in swift process, the unhappy woman obscured herself in some bushwood which abounded in the vicinity and seizing the advantage that a little time must elapse before the preventive efforts could avail to thwart the rash intention, she availed herself of the interim, afforded thus and plunged into the icy water of the stream, which consummated in the fatal and deplorable result, that minutes afterwards the would-be rescuers, who had made every effort to rescue and save her from so terrible a fate recovered the frail earthly tenement in which the vital spark was extinguished. The transmission of this occurrence, sad and deplorable as it is in its result, has shocked the conscience of the community, and filled it with sorrow and regret. In a supreme crisis like the one under consideration it is not the result, or the verdict elicited by a judicial enquiry, not always in harmony with the facts of the case, that we are most concerned, or are solicitous about. The object of the enquiry should be to thoroughly probe the case and ascertain its salient points. And thus reasoning, we ask could this deplorable tragedy by any human device have been averted? This poor woman for a long period had suffered undoubtedly from some acute form of mania, i.e. melancholia, or hysteria. She was excitable and highly nervous and there were many evidences of a mentality not altogether unpreventable, there were lucid intervals of considerable lengths, but on the other hand there were times of mental depression bordering upon despair and it is self evident, that in one of these moods the regrettable and deplorable result culminated.

Upon this same morning, somewhat later, a recurrence in the person of an elderly man, residing at Port Union, occurred. For some period previously he had been the victim of a somewhat aggravated mentality, conjuring up within himself various absurd hallucinations, the products of a morbid mind from which he could not be dissuaded. The climax was reached upon the morning in question, when he announced his intention of leaving the house, to which he never returned, for a while. It appears he walked to the railway wharf shouted "Here goes" and plunged into the shallow sea water, from which a few minutes later his body was rescued by some who were in close vicinity to the spot from whence he had leaped to his destruction. Upon its recovery the pockets of the coat were found to be weighed with iron.

Correspondent.

Catalina, May 26th, 1924.

It is a pleasure to turn from this distressing subject to a joyous one—a wedding. The event took place at Safe Harbor, on February 26, 1926; and was reported in the *Fisherman's Advocate,* published at Port Union, Newfoundland, in the issue of March 19, 1926.

WEDDING BELLS

ATTWOOD-DAVIS

On Thursday, January 21st, the people of our little village were aroused by the sound of wedding bells, and here and there the people could be seen dropping their work and hastening towards the church to witness the marriage of Mr. Purcy Attwood and Miss Priscilla Davis. About 3.30 the bride and groom entered the church. The bride leaning on the arm of her brother, Mr. Edgar Davis, while the groom was supported by his sister, Mrs. John G. Davis, and followed by two other bride boys and girls.

The wedding march was played as the party proceeded up the aisle of the church towards the altar, to take the solemn vows that were to unite them for life. The bride dressed in light fawn, with white bridal veil, adorned with Orange Blossoms, looked very attractive. Standing beside her was the gallant groom dressed in a suit of light.

The ceremony was performed by Rev. G. L. Mercer, after which the party proceeded towards the house of the groom's father, Mr. Thomas Attwood, where tea was being served for the bridal party. At 6 p.m. tea was again served for the guests, and an enjoyable party it was. The bride was the recipient of many useful and costly presents. Being organist of the church for twelve years, she was presented by the choir with four handsome carpet mats.

The moon shone gloriously upon the land at night, as the sun shone in the day, even nature seemed to be paying due respect to the happy bride, yet onlookers seemed to notice some little streak of sadness cross her face on giving up her maiden name and home.

The bride was the daughter of Mr. and Mrs. William Davis, an old and respected couple of our settlement. I daresay there was some little heartache at the parting of their daughter from them. Yet, she can smile on him through her tears, who undoubtedly wipes away the tears, and whispers in her ear; "Be

177

cheerful wife, I'll be more to you than all else has ever been."

At midnight the party disbursed for their different homes. Before going showers of congratulations were bestowed upon Mr. and Mrs. Attwood. The bride has secured for herself a handsome and devoted husband, the groom has chosen a fitting housewife, and a charming mistress. So while the moonlight was shining on the home and the love light was shining into their hearts all retired, leaving the happy couple alone to anticipate in their future happiness.

One of the Guests.

Safe Hr., February 26, 1926.

That is very graphic, and, I think, adequate. Let not the metropolitan press scorn the somewhat flowery language of the report, which is suited to the occasion, and is surely to be preferred to the more concise note on a similar event that appeared in the St. John's *Daily News* of June 26, 1926. It is true that in the latter the main facts are stated precisely, and there is even room—such has been the condensation—for a brag that the newspaper knew well beforehand what was to come off. But every lover of fine writing, and of human beings, must prefer the details of the rural account to the almost brutal brevity of the city-made paragraph.

WEDDING BELLS

According to time as arranged, and also previously announced in the *News,* the union of Miss Dorothy   and Mr. Silas   was consummated at the bride's home exactly at noon on Wednesday, the 23rd June. Rev. W. B. Bugden was the officiating minister.

The next item appeared on the front page of the *Western Star,* published at Curling, Bay of Islands, Newfoundland, in its issue of April 28, 1926. The village of Codroy, that is reported as suffering from inadequate ferry service, is somewhat back from the coast. "E.D.G.'s" letter proves the desire of the inhabitants to dignify discussions of public matters by employing lofty English. One almost forgets that the writer is only asking for an annual grant of eighty gallons of gasoline.

FERRY MATTERS IN CODROY VALLEY

Dear Sir, We regret that science has been playing Rip Van Winkle with us so long that we find ourselves not capable of offering to the transportation of our cattle and produce as commendable a passage over the floods as did our friend Noah over four thousands years ago, since he was never obliged to get out and push.

Our Searston ferry service is conducted by one man and an ungainly scow, square at both ends, whose only claim to the distinguished class of tenements constructed for man's use upon the sea is that it floats. And to think that in this progressive age, such a mass of soggy slabs with its load must be towed by a single man with oars, betrays an origination over whose mossy memories there has crept the improvements of many centuries. Not that we find fault with the scow itself, but to point out how difficult it is for a man to tow such a thing, that is encumbersome of necessity, since it must freight horses with their load against tide and wind, this Government service is not fat enough to have been fed upon the taxes, its lean and hungry look, its bone spavined razor back condition are the glaring symptoms of its having been kept in existence too long by the chaff of the revenue. We now ask our Government to remove this hideous imposition upon helpless humanity, by responding favorably to our petition for eighty gallons of gasoline yearly, the ferry-man having purchased a motor boat and engine at his own expense. Surely this would necessitate but a trivial expenditure considering the slavery it would eliminate, the time it would save, and the increased traffic it would tend to accommodate.

This is the appeal of outraged humanity, and we sincerely hope it will find humanitarian principles among those who are of the people, by the people and for the people. Thanking you for space, Mr. Editor, we are,

Sincerely,

E.D.G.

Codroy, April 19, 1926.

Here the tendency just illustrated finds possibly better, and certainly fuller, expression in the communication from E. W. Gillis, also of Codroy. This appeared in the *Evening Telegram* of St. John's on May 14, 1926. If it were prefaced by the salutation, "Men of Athens!" one might believe that Pericles or Demosthenes had dictated it.

CODROY'S COMPLAINTS

Editor *Evening Telegram*:

Dear Sir,—

"The humblest citizen in the land when clad in the armour of righteous cause is stronger than all the hosts of error." How much more worthy of attention then is the righteous cause of our combined people before whose individual judgment will eventually stand those responsible for the deplorable condition of our roads and bridges here.

It is really too disgusting for words that the efforts of our local Road Board to solicit the co-operation of the proper authorities to repair our roads and bridges have hopelessly failed. Now this is too bad. It has seen fit to obstruct Broom's Bridge as a precaution against a possible and very probable accident which

180

might horrify the whole country at its import. This bridge is in the middle of one of our central thoroughfares. The people are of necessity crossing despite the caution of the local Board. Now since they have done their utmost who will be responsible if human life is snuffed like candles from mangled tenements which today are breathing lively creatures, whose bodies may be extricated from a mass of foundered, rotten timber as evidence of the neglect of someone, and whose souls will speed on to accuse someone before the bar of eternal justice. Who is going to be accused? Ryan's Bridge has also been consigned by Father Time to the man-trap class, and we hear of another on the block road.

The roads are also practically impassable. In fact transportation facilities are far beneath the demands of primitive civilization, and unless we are going to return to the days of packing produce to the station on our back; slightly modernized by now having to swim the intervening rivers, well, it is time something was being done.

To add insult to injury the few men who had heart enough to bring cars to the locality are being forced to pay taxes. I have known these men to spend $25.00 of their private funds at a time to make the roads fit on which to put their cars. I have seen those cars sink in the middle of those roads which are a disgrace to a civilized country. The mud guards, the most serviceable part and, in the absence of propellers, regardless of traffic laws they must stay, their bottoms resting on the muck until rescued by the propelling force of the nearest farm horse. This was in the balmy days when the bridges were good, but now neither roads nor bridges are passable. In justice to our hereditary rights as free agents, the most priceless heritage of humanity, should those men pay taxes until the roads are so repaired as to warrant safety of travel? It is indeed a tax to put cars on the muck lanes we call by the usurped name of roads in this area.

The optimist who can trace one just motive through such procedure and bring it to a plausible conclusion is indeed deserving of being placed in the category of individuals whose delicate faculties of perception characterize them as being super-humanly endowed to discern the finest threads of justice interwoven with the injustice and neglect from which we are suffering.

We are watching St. George's and many outport districts are worthy of more consideration than they are getting. We are not saddling the blame on our Member, but I hope this might bring to his attention some of the things of which we stand very much in need and of which he may not be aware.

"Our liberties we prize, our rights we will maintain." We will marshal the whole public in support of our just demands. "All constituted authority emanates from the people and in the last resort must directly or indirectly be sanctioned or condemned by them according as its use or misuse may dictate."

Sincerely yours,

E. W. Gillis.

Codroy, May 6, 1926.

The following inspiring message saw print on February 3, 1926, also in the columns of the esteemed *Evening Telegram* of St. John's. I recognize its merits as prose; but my emotional response cannot be all it should, because of my disappointment over the honour of discovery not falling to Mr. Robins, who lives "at Random." No prospector ever chose a more suitable post office address, and the kind angels, who arrange these things, should have let him discover the mine.

ANOTHER MINERAL DEPOSIT UNEARTHED

Editor *Evening Telegram.*

Dear Sir,—Among the many topics it is the privilege of the press to discuss, no particular one, it seems to me, merits the consideration as that which tends to promote the welfare of our country and to correct in so far as it discovers to us the results possible our admitted self-conscious negligence.

May I, therefore, take occasion to set forth briefly through the medium of your esteemed journal a few facts in connection with what is now regarded by many prominent in the activities of our island as the Goshen of Newfoundland, and to arouse, if possible, in those interested in her development a spirit similar to that responsible for the discovery of this acquisition. It was believed originally to have been discovered by Mr. Robins, who resides at present at Random, and is now actively engaged in the progress of the work. The mineral deposit of which I speak is a high test quality of galena, and is situated at Hatchet Cove, Trinity. It has been unearthed through the personal efforts of Mr. Daniel Colford, well known as a prospector.

Leaving St. John's in the early part of May, Mr. Colford arrived at Hillview, Trinity, whence after a short stay he set out for the scene of his activities. But nature, as if conspiring with preconceived determination to thwart his designs, burst into a veritable tornado, pouring down upon the earth thick volumes of sleet and hail. Before him stretched a vast expanse of barren waste, interspersed with bogs and swamps, which in the gloom of the sweeping storm presented, to say the least, a rather discouraging aspect.

Suffice it to say that despite this atmospheric intervention he reached the goal of his desire, where little effort soon yielded a gratifying compensation, for there lying before his delighted gaze was a seam of gleaming mineral. Quickly procuring samples he returned to St. John's, where analysis showed the surprising percentage of 82.36 lead and 0.001 p.c. silver. Pleased with the success of his efforts thus far he again set to procure further samples for analysis in order to verify this gratifying result. Convinced at length that he possessed a genuine deposit of valuable mineral, he duly registered the claim and set about to develop it. It is now progressing favourably, though under adverse conditions, and a shipment of about sixty tons or more is expected to be made very soon to parties interested.

I jot down these few words merely to show the hidden forces that brought to light by such as Colford will without doubt elevate us from our present unenviable condition to the pedestal of independence.

Very truly yours,

Citizen.

The Gillises are public spirited. The final selection contains the moving appeal of Edwin D. Gillis, of Codroy (probably he who complained about the ferry), for the erection of a hospital on the West Coast; and sage advice as to its location. Proud as I am to have found a contribution of this quality, it must not be thought that I place the Newfoundland Gillises as high as James D. While they have talents of no mean order, he has genius of a unique variety. Still, there is a certain family resemblance that makes the harangues of the Newfoundland Gillises well worth preserving.

THE HOSPITAL

THE PORT IN THE STORM OF ILL-HEALTH

Editor *Evening Telegram.*

Dear Sir,—"Man's inhumanity to man makes countless thousands mourn." 'Tis so! The banners of selfishness, of greed and avarice float upon the airs of peace and war alike. In all nations and among peoples of practically every walk of life. This fact illuminates by comparison the exceptions where the sparks of humanitarianism still kindle into warmth and comfort the geniality and kindness which shine like golden stars upon the horizon of suffering and distress.

"A man will smile and bid you hail, yet wish you to the devil; but when a good dog wags his tail you know he's on the level." And so it is in the world today, while we can wade through obstacles to our objective. Supposing it be "through slaughter to a throne," the world applauds, our friends acclaim. But just as we reach the pinnacle of success, let ill-health smite us and note the fall. When we are no longer a machine in the money-making schemes of men, they but look to whoever is to take our places so that the broken cogs in the mechanism of their schemes be replaced, in order that they may conduct their pursuit of the mighty dollar as usual. This is but a logical compliance with the laws that underlie the maintenance and continuance of in-dustrial development upon which the very endurance of nations depend.

So there should be some place to which wrecked humanity can turn for solace and a fighting chance to live when they can no longer fight the battles of life. And each community should have its hospital, the haven of wrecked humanity, the most noble lay institution of which mother earth can boast. There we find skilled men and women devoting their lives daily to the allevia-tion of suffering. There the surgeon's knife roots lingering death from the vitals of poor sufferers and sends them on to bide their time upon the shores of fate.

'Tis true. "One touch of nature makes the whole world akin." Here more glaringly conspicuous than any place we know by the impost of reality is the idea of the poet: "The boast of heraldry, the pomp of power, and all that beauty, all that wealth e'er gave await alike the inevitable hour—the paths of glory lead but to the grave." Here sympathy begets sympathy and rich and poor alike stand equal chance of conquering that proud death which holds his narrow courts alike upon the fevered brow within the humblest hut or "within the hollow sceptre that rounds the mortal temples of a king." So that a proposed hospi-tal project anywhere should arouse the enthusiasm and gain the support of every individual in the locality regardless of class or creed.

We have had occasion to express our approval of the pro-posed hospital for the West Coast. More heartily than ever we highly endorse the scheme and solicit support in its behalf. It would be such a great thing for us all. Why cannot we all agree? There is a controversy as to where it should be built. We think there is but one logical answer to make. Put it in a place adapted by climate and surroundings to the cause of the sick room. If all denominations are to help finance it, it must be as near as possible to a place where all denominations are represented by their respective clergymen, and in conclusion, first considering the two above requisites, put it as nearly central as possible. In all events it is simply an investment to save life, let us to arms and show the humanitarian principle together with the independent spirit of the West. Thanking you for space, Mr. Editor, I am,

Sincerely yours,

Edwin D. Gillis.

Codroy, Dec. 12, 1926.

Poets of An Old Tradition

For Burns with glory did endow
And wove a garland round the plow.
—*James McIntyre.*

BRITISH LITERATURE OWES MUCH OF ITS SPLENDOR AND durability to its faithfulness to its ancient sources. Like all other national or racial literatures of north-western Europe, it had its rise in the hosts of the minstrels, who began their picturesque existence far back, beyond the reach of the oldest chronicles. Philosophic, and other forms of intellectualized poetry, like the work of Browning and John Donne, have exerted profound influence for comparatively short periods, and have then remained only as little used trails for the student to explore. But the lyric impulse, and the story-telling faculty, have never lost their potency. These form the base of all enduring British poetic literature; and when both reached their highest and completest expression in Shakespeare, its scholars crowned that bard as the world's greatest literary genius, and the popularity of his work is limited by nothing but the degree of literacy.

The democratic nature of British poetry is another aspect of the inheritance from the minstrels. Accompanying themselves on the harp, or some ruder instrument, they chanted their tales to the peasantry as well as to the king or baron in hall. The baron's hall was a good place to get a meal; but the minstrels wandered about the country, being restless souls and fond of the beauties of Nature; and when travelling they must needs eat, and were as ready to entertain the poor man as the king: they loved to sing, and they loved their songs, and they loved an audience. We find the minstrels with the armies in the field; and the Vikings' ships were rowed to lusty tunes, carolled free from bearded throats. Every one enjoys a story, and nearly every one likes a tune: so, while the minstrels did not get rich in lands or flocks or gold, they had as many meals as anybody else, and as good places to sleep.

The tales were generally of kings or knights, and fair ladies. Cynics think this is because the songmaker was looking for an extra draught of mead; and this may have been so: some singers aspired also to the permanent post of jester in the baronial retinue. But, self-seeking apart, what more romantic subjects were there than the bolder deeds of leaders, who had been chosen for strength and bravery? The pacific tiller of the soil would like to hear of battles, perhaps even more than the soldiers who had been in them, or people have changed strangely in their tastes. War and love and the hunt, and the greatest persons they knew about, woven into melodic narratives—these formed the stock in trade of the minstrels, and on their wit and skill depended their fortunes.

Strong racial characteristics are soonest lost, or submerged, or veneered over, by the aristocracy and by scholars, the former through personal association with members of other races, the latter by means of indirect association with foreigners through writings. With the spread of education, there began to be poets who got their inspiration from earlier books, instead of directly from the common fund of human experience, and who addressed their work to the understanding of scholars like themselves. Obviously, their poems did not reach the multitude in their first form. The value of their labours lay in the profundity of their thought, which, if vital enough, sooner or later stirred some other writer, who diluted the thought, and rephrased it in the vulgar tongue. Others, equally educated, stuck to the racial literary highway of the tune and the story, and, if competent at their trade, attained popularity. Among such we have Chaucer, Tennyson and Byron.

With the increasingly concentrated mental life of the great intellectual centres, there has been a tendency in the British poets to write more definitely for the intellectual classes, now numerous enough to furnish a wide public in themselves. The eleven hundred living poets in the British Isles, who have published volumes, would attain fair circulations if each purchased the books of the others; but it is doubtful whether any great proportion of them would attract the masses, in whom the love of the ballad and the short lyric persists undiminished.

At the same time, down under all this enormous body of intellectualized poetry, there has been continued the great tradition of the minstrels, that poetry should be simple and grow out of the more memorable things in common experience; that any one with natural talent and a yearning to do so may make poetry; and that the poetry so made is primarily for home consumption, to be directly communicated to immediate associates and acquaintances—not printed in a far place, and picked up by curious strangers in the proportion of one to ten thousand or a hundred thousand of the population.

Ignored—indeed, unsuspected—by the literary intellectuals, an army of such poets exists today in Canada, by their labours emphasizing the fact that the realm of poetry is not a closed preserve for the college-bred; but belongs equally to the humblest bard who cares to enter it, and is for the delight of the farmhand no less than of the emancipated young lady, smoking a surreptitious cigarette in a fashionable boarding-school. In thousands of villages and hamlets the local poet is as familiar a figure as the post-master.

Here, under other skies, and in different social and economic conditions, they perform the time-honoured functions of the minstrels of old—making verses to celebrate weddings, and to console those bereaved by the loss of loved ones; to mark great events, and to embellish with their art all kinds of public gatherings. James McIntyre was called on frequently to read his poems at socials and picnics; and, though a Presbyterian, he accepted the invitation of the Methodists to deliver a dedicatory ode at the opening of a new parsonage. Gay, an Anglican, was probably offering congratulations on the erection of a new church when he wrote *A Friendly Advice for the Baptist People*. Could any one be more the mouthpiece of his community than McIntyre was, not only in his cheese odes, but also in his lengthy narrative poems telling of the struggles of the pioneers, which he and his hearers had themselves experienced? The list of instances is endless; but we must include Gillis's remarks on the inception of *The Cape Breton Giant* as a splendid example of the celebration of a local hero:

The writing of this work was suggested by Murdoch MacLean, of Upper East Ainslie. The author had seen an article in the *Family Herald and Weekly Star* about Angus MacAskill. In a colloquy which this suggested, Mr. MacLean said, "it would be a grand idea to write a life of MacAskill." The Author soon took up the matter, and this book is the result.

At home, the local poet is a man of mark, esteemed by his fellows, and wearing his honours with dignity, and generally with modesty. It will have been observed that three of the four major studies in this volume are of Scottish poets—Caledonian bards, as they love to be called. The predominance of the Scot in this high calling is due to the number of that race who have happily been led to our shores; to the especial love of the Gael for melody and learning; and to the noble example of Robert Burns—the plough-boy who became the greatest hero of his nation, and whose illustrious career has encouraged others of lowly station to try their hands at rhyming. The foreword to James MacRae's *Poems* of 1877 strongly supports this view. In modesty, it equals the apology of McIntyre, formerly quoted. Also, MacRae's claim for the freedom of the poetic realm to peer and peasant is strikingly in harmony with the main argument of this essay:

TO THE PUBLIC

In submitting the following poems to your judgment, the author does so in a truly Christian spirit—that is with fear and trembling, knowing how few of those who think they are called to be authors enter in at the narrow gate which leads to fame—the only reward for which any one worthy of the name of author labours as such.

The author thinks that the present case has a claim to your especial indulgence; for the deed to be judged (good, evil or indifferent, as it may be) is that of a person whom fortune, with all its attendant blessings (and let us trust its curses too) has sadly neglected and forced to seek for the scanty education and information necessary for the performance of the work outside of the usual channels, and by devoting thereto the few hours which hard manual labour allows for recreation and amusement. But lest this should go to show that it was an impertinence on his part to attempt the task at all, it must be borne in mind that poetry is the pure gift of nature which she bestows on whom she pleases; rich and poor, learned and unlearned, share her

192

favours alike. Burns as peasant, and Byron as lord, were equally recipients of her bounty.

With these remarks, I humbly submit myself to any sentence you may be pleased to pass.

J. J. M.

Possibly improved means of transport and communication has already marked the local bard for extermination. If so, the country will be the poorer; and it is to be hoped that some real effort will be made to perpetuate the memory of this picturesque type. It is a never-to-be-forgotten experience to hear one of these village Homers reading his poems in a solemn, sonorous voice, with finely controlled passion and flashing eye. In the late eighties and nineties, when the tribe flourished most abundantly, the scene would be lit by an oil lamp, and the well-defined features of the reader's face would be softened by masses of hair above the wide brow, and masses of beard shading the lower part of the face, and obscuring the neck.

MacRae, who has heard of the thinning ranks of the "rustic bards" in Scotland, mourns the silent glens that were once filled with the sound of the bagpipes, and the dreary cottages no longer enlivened by the recital of home-made ballads:

> The Gaelic tongue, to them so dear,
> Whose charming strains so sweet and clear,
> Supplied good music to the ear,
>   And warmed the heart,
> The stranger there can seldom hear
>   In any part.

193

The rustic bards no longer raise
Their voices sweet in Gaelic lays
To sing in melodies the praise
        Of lord or chief;
The bagpipes pass their nights and days
        In silent grief.

The more primitive life to which the Canadian Scots came is responsible for the continuance of the type here in great numbers. He is most apt to be found in the remoter sections; and will not pass until the terrible day when all the villages know the same artificial life as the cities. A recent traveller in Cape Breton reports the discovery of one while taking a drive in the vicinity of South East Margaree:

> D. D. McFarlane is full of local poetry, which seems to have been composed by a cousin of his, an old man who is now not very well. He is a fine man and willing to do anything to bring his beloved "New Scotland" into prominence. He recited several little verses from time to time during the drive, relative to some of the local mountains, glens and streams, and all of these certainly had a fine thread in them.

As one recalls Loch Lomond and Melrose Abbey, and other names beyond count in British poetry, which stand for the love of a local scene, transmuted by the poet's art into an integral part of our racial heritage; he will not scoff at the power of the local to move the whole nation, and even persons of other nationality; but will be anxious for the day when every Canadian plain and peak and lake wins immortal life in song or story. The local poets have a great work to do, even if their verses only teach the people of their own communities to venerate the hills by which they are surrounded.

The four Jameses belong definitely to the ranks of the local poets. Yet they are not typical of their class; for the reason that they transcended that class, and became national poets. Many of the characteristics of the local poet are found in the work of one or other of the four. There is much, too, in the characters of the four that reminds one of the genuine local poet. This is not surprising since they all began their careers in that capacity. More than one of them was so deeply marked with the traits of local poets that he continued to exhibit those traits long after he had ceased, in any real sense, to be a local poet himself. Indeed, some of those traits were too deeply implanted to be shaken off at all.

The Jameses, in short, are brilliant exceptions, whose extraordinary individual powers forced them out of the comfortable obscurity of their positions as local seers and singers, and thrust them into the national arena, where their differences from the other national poets are as clearly defined as their genius has definitely cut them off from their one-time peers, the village poets. Differing as we have seen that they do from each other in temperament, outlook, mental processes and

artistic methods, they are yet united as a somewhat
lonely little group in the literary No Man's Land.

Nobody seems to know just how to treat them.
They have won their audiences, thanks to nothing but
their natural gifts. And it is a high achievement to have
pleased readers for nearly half a century, as Gay has
done, or, like Gillis, from an obscure point on the Mar-
gareee River, to have made one's self felt over half the
earth. Yet the critics, for reasons that can be understood rather than sympathized with, have ignored the
little band, whose fame continues to spread without the
sympathetic interest of literary coteries.

To continue to ignore them is as impossible as it is
unwise. Their work is unique, and will continue to
attract readers over an indefinite period. However
much our academic friends may disapprove, the Jameses
have become a part of the distinctive national literary
tradition. If they are hard to classify, that is a problem for criticism; and the originality of a literary figure
was never yet sufficient cause for ignoring him, though
that has often been tried by critics during the early
parts of the careers of exceptional writers.

These men should be classed together, and not iden-
tified either with the village poets from whom they
sprang, nor yet with the academic-national poets, from
whom they differ just because they began as village
poets. In the group made up of themselves, they form
a quartette, in whose performances Canada may take

pride. That does not mean they should be treated as winners of a race in which there are no other contestants. Their kind is known elsewhere, and comparisons are possible. In 1829 Robert Southey, the English poet and prose writer, discovered the species; and proceeded to write *Lives of the Uneducated Poets,* which is still in print. If that useful work be consulted, the student may assure himself that our four Jameses are more interesting, more ingenious, and more forceful writers than the English John Jones, whom Southey puts forward as the English champion in their class.

Pending the issue of a book dealing with the work of the local poets, the sketches of the Jameses in this volume will serve to familiarize the reader with some of the characteristics of local poetry, of which only one need be mentioned here. That is the breadth and diversity of experience out of which local poetry grows. In reply to a taunt that he could not be much of a writer because he had not visited Europe, Thoreau replied: "I have travelled much—in Concord." The local poets have learned a great deal of the basic activities of the nation at first hand. To indicate concretely what this means, I list the vocations represented, at some time or other, by merely the four chief figures in this book: carpenter, gun-smith, saw-filer, hotel-keeper, showman, furniture-maker, merchant, sugar-maker, undertaker, farmer, surveyor, sawmill-hand, attendant in lunatic asylum, school teacher, watchman and labourer. On an average, each of them had practical knowledge of four callings; and in venturing to speak for one's fellowmen it is some advantage to have handled a shovel or pitch-fork with them.

There is one more word to be said. It covers both the Jameses and their lesser brethren, the local poets. As a body, they are the voice of the pioneers; and there is an increasing feeling in this country, which does the people credit, that there is no more sacred word in the Canadian vocabulary than pioneers. Reason, as well as filial duty, makes us hold them in honour. They came to this country bringing what they had, which was usually only themselves, their families, their hope, their faith and determination. They engaged upon the longest battle in history—the Battle of the Wilderness, by no means without its casualties; and they won it decisively after a century of unremitting struggle. It is more fittingly a matter for pride to have had an ancestor who swung an axe in that battle, than a more remote one who plied his axe at Crecy or Agincourt. It was men like McIntyre, who gave themselves without stint, who did the best they knew how and endured whatever sacrifices that entailed, that made possible not only our material prosperity, but set standards of Canadian character and conduct which the younger generation, with all the advantages it has inherited from the pioneers, has not noticeably surpassed. They are not the ones to begrudge their descendants their places of intellectual superiority from which they look down on the simplicity of their forefathers: the pioneers worked to that very end. When the limitations of an old warrior like McIntyre are apparent, it is sanity and not sacrilege to smile at them; but it should be done kindlily, remembering always their inescapable disadvantages, their valor and their chivalry.

Manifesting differently, conditioned in its utterance by the outward circumstances of the individual life, the poet nature is inherently the same everywhere and in all ages. The poet is one who comprehends life through the emotions rather than the intellect. He does not analyze experience, like the philosopher, but assimilates and interprets it by the involuntary responses of his own being. He speaks from the heart to the heart; and the head will never wholly understand the heart, any more than the heart will ever enter joyously, or even contentedly, into all the crafty designs of the head. The poet is dedicated from birth to the service of Beauty and Love and Ideals, that are often at variance with prudent concerns for material well-being and advancement; and, because this world is still a rough and miry place, the poet must often wander wistful as a child, and lonely as the cloud to which he instinctively turns his eyes to avoid the sight of some form of unloveliness, designed for merely practical ends. Yet, for all his apparent isolation from men, he feels as no other the inner yearning of Man, and it has been largely through his eyes that men have perceived the great spiritual laws that make life bearable, and in his company that they have found the verdure-bordered vistas, whose end is Peace.

The real key to the understanding of the men introduced in this book is that they share this nature. Their aspirations, their will to universal betterment, and their intuitive reach beyond the measure of their grasp, is easily traceable through their writings, like the proverbial thread of gold. By these they shall be judged and not by flaws in the pattern. The more their work is pondered, the greater one's affection for them, the greater his admiration for their honest efforts to noble expression, and the greater his tolerance for mistakes, growing out of inevitable limitations of opportunity, and creating the human, personal touches that first attract readers to them. Who sees not this, has lost the better, sweeter half of their message, and is himself to blame.

Bibliography

BIBLIOGRAPHY

JAMES GAY

Poems by James Gay, Poet Laureate of Canada, Master of All Poets. Written while Crossing the Sea in 1882. 6¼ x 4¼ inches, 18 pages, blue paper covers. Published at Guelph, Ontario, 1883. Out of print.

Canada's Poet: Yours alway, James Gay; Poet Laureate of Canada & Master of All Poets, this day. Introduction by James Millington. 5½ x 4¼ inches, 87 pages, plus 15 pages of Addenda. Light buff paper covers. Published at one shilling by Field & Tuer at Ye Leadenhalle Presse, London, E.C., England; Simpkin, Marshall & Co.; Hamilton, Adams & Co., 1884 or 1885. Out of print.

JAMES McINTYRE

Musings on the Banks of the Canadian Thames by James McIntyre. Published in 1884. Out of print.

Poems of James McIntyre. "Fair Canada is our Theme, Land of rich Cheese, Milk and Cream." 6 x 8½ inches, 195 pages, portrait of the author, red cloth covers. Published at the office of The Chronicle, Ingersoll, Ontario, 1889. Out of print.

Rhymes Right or Wrong of Rainy River by Kate McIntyre Ruttan. 6¾ x 5 inches, 182 pages, stiff blue paper covers. Published by The Times Printing Company, Orillia, Ontario, 1926. Portraits of James McIntyre, Kate McIntyre Ruttan and others. To be had for $1 from Mrs. Kate McIntyre Ruttan, Lavalee, Ontario.

JAMES D. GILLIS

The Cape Breton Giant: A Truthful Memoir by Jas. D. Gillis. Published by John Lovell & Son, Montreal, 1898. Numerous reprints by T. C. Allen and Co., Halifax, Nova Scotia, 7 x 4¾ inches, 95 pages, pink or brown paper covers. Portraits of the author, and of Angus MacAskill and Tom Thumb. To be had for 43c post paid from T. C. Allen & Co., Halifax, Nova Scotia.

Modern English: "Leave the Old to Old." Canadian Grammar by James D. Gillis, Teacher, author of the C.B. Giant. Published by A. C. Bertram, Proprietor of North Sydney Herald, Nova Scotia, 1904. Reprints 7 x 4¾ inches, 65 pages, light brown paper covers, by T. C. Allen & Co., Halifax, Nova Scotia, at 43c post paid.

Four Pole Map of the World by James D. Gillis, Teacher. Blue Prints to be had from the author, South West Margaree, Nova Scotia, at $3.

The Great Election by James D. Gillis, Teacher, Author of the "C.B. Giant" and Canadian Grammar. Dedicated to Dr. A. H. McKay, Halifax. 6¾ x 4½ inches, light bluish-green paper covers, 43 pages. Published by the North Sydney Herald Job Print, 1915 or 1916. To be had from T. C. Allen & Co., Halifax, Nova Scotia, at 43c post paid.

A short work on his trip to Palestine.

JAMES MacRAE

Poems written by J. J. MacDonald, a Native of County Glengarry, Ont. 7 x 4¼ inches, 64 pages, blue paper covers. Published about 1877. To be had from the author, P.O. Box 184, St. Mary's, Ontario, at 25c.

An Ideal Courtship by James MacRae, 7¼ x 5 inches, 43 pages, blue cloth. Published by the Ryerson Press, Toronto, Ontario, 1923. To be had from the author, P.O. Box 184, St. Mary's, Ontario, at 60c.

Complete Poems, 1930.

ANASTASIA HOGAN

Selection of Poems by Anastasia Hogan, 6¾ x 5 inches, 143 pages, orchid paper covers. Printed by G. S. Milligan, Jr., St. John's, Newfoundland.

LILLIAN FORBES GUNTER

Loving Memories and Other Poems by Lillian Forbes Gunter, 7 x 5 inches, 45 pages, yellow paper covers. Printed by The Leader Publishing Company, Regina, Saskatchewan.